Praise for *Practicing Profitability*

"Without a doubt, Vericle is the best system going, period. Reports, SOAPs, posting of charges. Your system makes everything so smooth and efficient. Most docs don't realize how much they need this program and your services. Thank you so much for building it. I can't say enough."

—Curtis Fedorchuk, DC
Cumming, Georgia

"The findings in Vericle's data are actionable. Trends are traceable. The net results are measurable improvements in revenue, compliance, and overall efficiency."

—Michael Lagana, DC
BackSmart Wellness Center
Edison, New Jersey

"Vericle's technology is the backbone of my practice, which is now completely paperless. Vericle shows me a bird's-eye view of every practice I coach. It helps me objectively judge how much effort I should invest in each doctor-coach relationship to help many more people get the best possible care."

—Charles Majors, DC
Planet Chiropractic
Romeoville, Illinois

Practicing Profitability

Practicing Profitability

Billing Network Effect for Revenue Cycle Control in Healthcare Clinics and Chiropractic Offices

Collections, Audit Risk, SOAP Notes,
Scheduling, Care Plans, and Coding

Yuval Lirov

Affinity Billing Inc.
Marlboro, New Jersey

Affinity Billing Inc.
Marlboro, New Jersey

Library of Congress Cataloging-in-Publication Data
    Lirov, Yuval
Practicing Profitability: Billing Network Effect for Revenue Cycle Control in Healthcare Clinics and Chiropractic Offices / Yuval Lirov
      p.   cm.
    Includes bibliographical references and index
    ISBN 978-0-9796101-1-0
    1. Chiropractic—Medical—Practice Management, Billing, etc.

2007903656

First Edition, reissue with new subtitle 2007
Printed in the United States of America

Interior Book Design and Copyediting by Alison F. Cohen

To Shulamith, Victor, Mazal, Erez, Roy,
Reuven, Lori, and Danielle

Table of Contents

List of Figures

Foreword

The only failure the man should fear is the failure to do his best.

—D. D. Palmer (1845–1913)

I'm concerned about where the chiropractic profession is going in terms of profitability. I feel like most practice owners are indifferent and apathetic, while the ship is being steered by people who do not have our best interests at heart—out-of-control payers and incompetent billers, to name two. We are at an absolutely crucial and unprecedented point in our history where technology enables the insurance companies to underpay us, profile us, audit us, and take back the little money that was paid.

I decided to start Billing Precision because I needed a billing solution for my own practice. I had experienced second-rate service firsthand for too long, and I knew of no solution I could trust with the rapid development of my practice. I knew that lots of people felt the same way, but I could not wait anymore for somebody else to do it for me.

When I graduated from Life University, I continued my studies with some of the most influential doctors, including Dr. Lerner, Dr. Loman, and Dr. Nalda. In addition to outstanding clinical training, I also learned from them how to approach building and managing my own practice. I learned the importance of discipline and the potential of adequate infrastructure. I also saw how frustrated they were with the lack of integrated solutions; everything about running the office seemed to require memory management—from scheduling the patient to tracking care plan compliance to managing outstanding balances.

In many ways, working with practice owners reminds me of working with the patient; a practice is a very complex system, where the flow of information must be uninhibited in order to have the practice growing at a healthy pace. Patients must make progress, and vital functions of the office too must perform optimally to grow and to avoid risks.

A systemic "subluxation" may not be immediately observable to a naked and untrained eye, yet it may cause major setbacks for the practice owner. Just like patients who lack education about their own bodies and nervous systems, practice owners are often ignorant about the reasons for their underpayment or for the lack of practice growth.

My own viewpoints changed in step with the growing scope of our service. As the number and size of the practices we support grew, I realized that my initial conjecture about the importance of integrated office workflow is paramount to success. For instance, besides a solid billing process, perfect SOAP notes are critical for better care, for lower audit risk, and for full reimbursement.

Two other critical points are the practice owner's business focus and teamwork. An unfocused practice owner will always confuse profit, revenue, and costs. And insurance companies will always exploit the lack of teamwork between billing and front office personnel.

Today, I realize that focus and teamwork can be turned

around from being points of vulnerability to the strongest weapon for improving practice profitability and making the insurance companies pay everything they owe you. You can lock them down. You can research your options, fight back, and help others to fight back too.

By applying our solution, we transform disparate, stand-alone billing companies from the many into the mighty. Chiropractic clinic owners who use our solution are paid more, faster, and for less. I am lucky to be in a position to help on such a meaningful scale.

This book documents our experience and presents many of the concepts Vericle pioneered in a simple and pragmatic way—so that the chiropractor who sees 1,000 patients a week can improve practice workflow and profitability, and a chiropractor who sees 100 patients a week can accelerate her practice buildup tenfold.

—Brian Capra, DC
Billing Precision, LLC
Dumont, New Jersey

Acknowledgments

This book is a result of teamwork and hard work by several talented teams. Erez Lirov contributed countless ideas and led every aspect of system development and maintenance. Lori and Mazal Lirov worked right next to us, implementing it in practice. Roy Lirov contributed major portions of advertising and written and recorded training material. Dr. Doug Cassel introduced us to medical billing and, together with Bob Ettl, provided inspiration and support.

Hundreds of doctors, office managers, and lawyers generated a continuous flow of original requirements. Special thanks to Dr. Brian Capra, Director of Advanced Chiropractic; Dr. Zelik Frischer, clinical professor of urology at Stony Brook University School of Medicine; Dr. Ted Gutowski of Robert Wood Johnson University Hospital; Dr. Vivian Kominos of Heart Specialists of Central Jersey; Dr. Michael Lagana, director of BackSmart Wellness; Dr. Glenn Laub, chairman of cardiothoracic surgery at St. Francis Hospital in New Jersey; Drs. Ben Lerner and Greg Loman, co-founders of Maximized Living Inc.; Dr. Michael Lewko, chief medical officer at Care Management of St. Joseph Hospital; Dr. Charles Majors, director of Planet Chiropractic; Dr. Gamil Makar, director of Senior Health Partners; Dr. Michael McGinnis, chairman of surgical pathology at Centrastate Medical

Center; Dr. Sigmund Miller, executive director of the Association of New Jersey Chiropractors (ANJC); Dr. Anthony Nalda, director of Nalda Family Chiropractic; Dr. Boris Petrikovsky, chairman of the Department of Obstetrics & Gynecology at Nassau University Medical Center and professor of Obstetrics, Gynecology, and Reproductive Medicine at Stony Brook University School of Medicine; Jeffrey Randolph, ANJC legal counsel; and Dr. Robert White, director of True Health Chiropractic.

Finally, my sincere thanks and appreciation go to Alison F. Cohen, my editor, who brought with her the highest book publishing standards and book preparation project management skills and who dramatically improved both my grammar and the overall clarity and flow of my writing.

About This Book

Increasing complexity of billing creates opportunities for the payers to benefit at the expense of the providers. Endless claim denials, payment delays, and post-payment audits are all too familiar symptoms of dilettante billing. Doctors require professional solutions.

—Sigmund Miller, DC
Executive Director
Association of New Jersey Chiropractors

Your practice survives on its collections. Collections determine the value of your practice and define the difference between a thriving business and a sleepy or insolvent clinic.

According to the Office of Inspector General (OIG), an overall claims submission error rate in 2005 reached 67%, resulting in $285 million in improper payments (Office of Inspector General [OIG], 2006). Naturally, a similarly huge amount was also underpaid. This book shows simple, pragmatic ways to reduce both underpayment and overpayment risks.

This book is aimed at healthcare providers who are tired of substandard billing performance and are looking for proven ways of systematic payment performance improvement. It creates awareness of the payer-provider conflict, lists specific strategies and techniques payers use to keep providers' money, and then shows how to leverage the "network effect" for improving those all-important collections numbers and building profitable practices.

Who needs this book? *You* do, if you are . . .

- **A practice owner** who is losing sleep because of shrinking collections, growing audit risk, and escalating overhead
- **A coach** who is frustrated that members do not follow your direction and do not perform as well as expected
- **An owner of a billing service company** who is unable to profitably grow the business because of cutthroat offshore competition, talent scarcity, and escalating costs of personnel and technology
- **A practice manager** who is overwhelmed by thousands of billing service providers and armies of practice management consultants
- **A practice management consultant** who is intimidated by insurance companies and confused by hundreds of billing and electronic medical record (EMR) systems
- **A billing specialist** who is dreaming to start your own billing service and looking for a profitable business development and operating methodology
- **A medical coder** who is worried about the disappearing future of the coding specialty because of doctors using paper- or computer-based "superbills"
- **A healthcare practice compliance officer** who is

afraid of impending audit, fraud potential, security and privacy violations, or data loss

- **A computer programmer** who is tired of being underpaid—and who wants to transition to a lucrative medical records or billing technology software firm
- **A chiropractic student** who is about to start your own practice and who needs education about modern solutions to practice management challenges
- **A student in a graduate healthcare management or administration program** who plans to become a practice management consultant

The fact that you're reading this book means that you've probably already encountered some of these problems:

- **Lower billing performance**
    - Painfully slow collections
    - Frequent payment denials

- **Increasing audit risk**
    - Growing frequency of post-payment audits
    - Paying refunds and penalties

When we developed Vericle Billing System, it was a matter of professional survival. At the time, thousands of healthcare practices had separate billing systems. The result was thousands of small installations, all falling into the payer's methodology and leaving significant portions of the provider's money to the payer. We had to find a better way to collect payments than the stale, rote methods introduced by insurance companies that aim toward paying less and keeping the physician's money for themselves. Because of our expertise in applying Straight-Through

Processing (STP) methodology to telecommunications and financial management domains—which I documented in my earlier book, *Mission-Critical Systems Management* (Prentice Hall, 1997)—we focused on extending STP to healthcare. Our experiments extended far beyond developing new collections techniques. We gradually created Vericle, a comprehensive practice management system that includes billing process management tools and a completely new billing and practice management philosophy.

Vericle's system uses centralized technology that serves hundreds of stand-alone billing services and healthcare clinics. With its emphasis on centralized tracking of payer performance from a single point of control, shared coding compliance rules, and accountable teamwork, Vericle's system demonstrates the "network effect" and performance improvements to billing companies and physician practices around the country.

What Will This Book Do for You?

This book will not teach you the basics of practice management, coding, billing, or compliance. For introductory material, there are excellent texts listed at the back of this book (Aalseth, 1999; Buppert, 2005; Burgos, 2006; Delman, 2002; Reizer, 2002; Rowell & Green, 2005; Saner, 2000). Medical practice is a business, and doctors need to make strategic decisions about adding equipment, hiring other doctors, addressing specific kinds of patients, selection of referrals, marketing, etc. To learn how to use quantitative data to make such decisions, look up *The Business of Medical Practice: Advanced Profit Maximization Techniques for Savvy Doctors* (Marcinko, 2004).

Practicing Profitability takes over where these texts leave you; as you read this book, your view of billing will change. The

Vericle system transforms the nature of the claims processing cycle. It provides an accountable approach to billing that places the practice owner firmly in control. The book documents our experience and provides structured direction on how to apply it in practice to improve your revenue and office management productivity.

I chose chiropractic examples because of high processing volumes, low average claim payment value, and a uniquely high likelihood for audit. Together, these three aspects of chiropractic combine for especially demanding conditions in terms of office automation.

First, the average chiropractor sees many more patients than any other specialist, often exceeding the average family practice visit frequency by an order of magnitude. Chiropractic is the fastest-growing specialty in terms of Medicare reimbursements; it grew from 11.2 million services and $255 allowed in 1994 to 21 million services and $683 million allowed in 2004. Hence, simplistic SOAP note management and traditional electronic patient scheduling alone are not powerful enough for meaningful productivity improvements.

Next, at an average reimbursement of $28, 82% of chiropractors supplement their revenue with retail product sales at the point of service. So their billing software must be able to handle the widest range of financial arrangements, including insurance and cash payments, retail sales, and care plans.

Third, chiropractors face the highest rate of post-payment audits. Hence the special importance of audit risk and pristine SOAP note management techniques.

Chiropractors need the most sophisticated office management infrastructure, yet they have the least extra cash to afford it. In other words, the requirements for chiropractic office automation software are so uniquely demanding that any software capable of handling a chiropractic office with low maintenance costs can easily support most other specialties.

Most chapters in this book outline specific implementation steps. The best way to benefit from this book is to follow these steps in practice. Here's an example of how *Practicing Profitability* teaches you to evaluate billing performance: Take a sheet of blank paper and grab your last monthly billing report. On the paper, draw a graph, with the y-axis (vertical) showing percent as 0–100 and the x-axis (horizontal) showing time as 15, 30, 45, 60, 90, and 120 days. Next, draw a vertical bar on your graph at 15 days, to show the percentage of 15-day receivables, and at each subsequent time increment (Figure 1).

Figure 1. Payment Distribution Chart

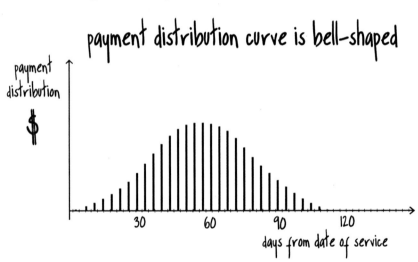

Payment distribution provides
visual indication of billing quality.

A tight, narrow bell curve centered around 10–15 days means that your billing service has excellent performance. A wide, flat bell curve centered around 60 or 75 days means that payers take advantage of your practice—and you're leaving a significant portion of your reimbursement to the payers (Part V).

I welcome your feedback to help me improve future editions of this book. Please email your comments and suggestions via the Contact Us page at www.vericle.net.

Practicing Profitability

Part I

Payer-Provider Conflict

Now, here, you see, it takes all the running you can do, to keep in the same place. If you want to get somewhere else, you must run at least twice as fast as that!

—The Queen
Through the Looking Glass
Lewis Carroll

Ideally, the billing encounter should be viewed as a win-win situation. But a practice owner or billing manager who has spent time "in the trenches" knows that this is simply not the case. Insurance companies have adopted an adversarial approach to providers. Under the payer's "system," the goal is to keep as much as possible of the provider's money without violating the timely payment laws. Payers can delay claims processing, underpay, return for payment refunds, and impose penalties.

Modern medical billing started in 1984, when the Health

Care Financing Administration (HCFA), now called the Centers for Medicare and Medicaid Services (CMS), first required providers to use the standard HCFA-1500 form and standard CPT codes to submit Medicare claims.

At first, HCFA forms were coded manually and submitted by mail, while the two key participants—namely, HCFA and Medicare—established the following reporting standards:

- 1988 – Medicare added the requirement to report ICD-9 on HCFA-1500 forms.
- 1989 – Medicare required all physicians to submit claims on behalf of Medicare patients, regardless of the physician's participation in the Medicare program.
- 1996 – HCFA developed Correct Coding Initiative (CCI) to promote national coding standards in terms of matching rules between ICD-9 and CPT codes.

Technology became the decisive weapon in the payer-provider conflict. Billing technology developed initially along three directions: data entry, claims processing (adjudication), and participant connectivity. By 1996, payers had already heavily invested in building electronic claims processing technology. Payers also almost completely eliminated their data entry costs by enabling electronic claims submissions and shifting claim coding costs to providers. To connect payers with providers and consumers, Jim Clark conceived Healtheon (now Emdeon), the first claims clearinghouse. Since its creation in 1996, Healtheon evolved into the largest electronic claims clearinghouse, connected to thousands of payers.

Given the high cost of software in the late 1990s, provider-side claims processing software could not keep up with payers' technology, and it remained limited to electronic claims submission. Thousands of providers resorted to feature-poor, client-server installations. These are costly to install and maintain and are unable to match the payer's processing power. Yet other industries, such as telecommunications and investment banking, developed processes for millions of transactions across multiple remote participants. Straight-Through Processing (STP) emerged as the leading methodology to keep up with regulatory demands and massive transaction volumes.

Vericle was born in 2001. It was envisioned as an enabling technology for providers to match the awesome processing power available to the largest payers. Its centrally managed platform integrates medical office billing and front office functionalities with Internet connectivity, leveraging STP methodology.

Vericle tracks payer performance from a single point of control and shares compliance rules globally. Vericle also takes advantage of Software as a Service (SaaS) delivery models, improving operations control, turning a capital expense into an operating expense, and therefore improving a practice's balance sheet.

A centrally managed STP platform delivered under the SaaS model was bound to culminate in a qualitative service change. Thus in 2004, Vericle began consolidating operations for hundreds of stand-alone billing services and practices, igniting the network effect: Vericle users began gaining more value in step with its growing network.

Chapter 1

What's Happened to Your Promising Practice?

You didn't go into healthcare to be "average." Like most good doctors, you're an optimist. You believe you can be a top producer and earn the highest possible compensation for your services. After all, you have excellent training and you're not afraid of hard work.

Yet your practice is not making what you think it should be making. What's gone wrong? And, more importantly, what, if anything, can you do about it?

This part examines **why billing services fail to collect as promised**. It looks at what keeps so many otherwise talented, capable practice owners and managers from generating top revenue.

The good news is that billing performance can be improved—dramatically and permanently. But first you need to know where to begin and what needs fixing.

If you're like most practice owners and managers who hit "low collections," you might blame your setbacks on insurance companies or billing personnel. Don't. By placing the blame elsewhere, you'll cheat yourself of a valuable opportunity to improve your profitability. Instead, take a good, hard, dispassionate look at what you're doing. Chances are you'll find that the fault lies somewhere within your office: your attitude, your processes, or your technology. Vericle research has shown this to be particularly true for practice owners or managers experiencing any of the following common billing problems:

- Insurance companies . . .
    - increase your denial rates
    - ignore your appeals
    - audit your medical notes and impose refunds and fines

- You . . .
    - lack consistent and integrated billing methodology
    - employ an incompetent and/or lazy billing service that collects fees on easily paid claims and forfeits difficult claims without follow-up
    - are unable to identify and discover specific reasons for specific underpayments

While the telltale signs of billing underachievement may appear countless, the true causes are generally quite specific, and their roots can be found in the overall approach you take to the billing process.

Chapter 2

Whose System Are You Following?

When two people tango, only one leads.
—Sign at dance studio

In the "provider-payer tango"—Vericle's metaphor for a claim-payment interaction—there are always two systems at work: the provider's system and the payer's system. To lead in this process, you must have and use a billing system that works. Merely submitting claims and then placing yourself in the arms of the payer, waiting to get paid, is not enough.

Healthcare insurance businesses continued to boom in 2006, mostly at the expense of both providers and patients. Two key aspects dominate the business background for insurers in 2006:

1. **Insurers must meet tougher profit margin benchmarks.** For instance, UnitedHealthcare saw its earnings rise 38% in the third quarter of 2006 alone (Moore, 2007). To keep its share value growing, UnitedHealthcare will have to demonstrate still better

performance in the third quarter of 2007.

2. **Insurers approach the limit of their ability to grow premiums.** In 2001–2006, premiums increased disproportionately compared to inflation and workers' earnings growth. For instance, health insurance premiums increased 65.8% between 2001 and 2006, while inflation grew 16.4% and workers' earnings increased 18.2% during the same period (Moore, 2007) (Figure 2).

Figure 2. Disproportionate Growth of Insurance Premiums

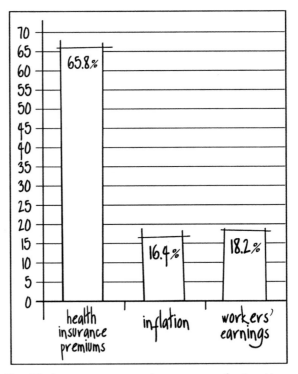

Health insurance premiums grow faster than inflation and workers' earnings.

The motive in business is always profit, but insurance companies have it particularly rough. They play in a massively regulated, traditionally altruistic industry, where they are the only for-profit game in town. Against all odds, they aggressively pushed their way to the top. But now, as Wall Street sweethearts, they have stepped through the looking glass into a world that seems to keep pace, no matter how fast they run. The faster they grow profits, the higher they drive expectations, leaving them increasingly desperate for new ideas to generate revenue.

Practice owners and billing service managers must assume responsibility for the current sad state of provider-payer relations. The efficacy of your system determines whether you lead or follow in the provider-payer tango. To take control, you must know what's happening at each step. You also must be comfortable in a leadership role. Vericle's research shows that most practice owners and managers struggle, and often fail, because they don't know how to be in control of the payment process.

Payers develop their current system in response to their business needs. Fair or unfair, the onus is on the provider/billing service, not the insurer. Rather than complain, you have to learn to thrive within the insurer's constraints. If the insurer's system can derail your billing efforts, then you need to adopt a modern, more effective billing system. It's that simple.

This book shows a better way. You may not get every claim paid—however, by using our system, you'll get more claims paid and you'll certainly know what's happening to each one at every step. But first, you must understand how and why the payer's system works so well.

Chapter 3

The Payer's System

Payers have developed a simple but effective bag of tricks to seize control of and rapidly derail a significant portion of billing efforts. They typically employ these strategies:

1. Increase billing service costs with added complexity and new denial reasons.
2. Reduce allowed fees.
3. Increase leverage over providers through consolidation.
4. Underpay claims.
5. Return for post-payment audits, demand refunds, and impose penalties.

Strategy I: Increase Billing Service Costs with Added Complexity and New Denial Reasons

Payers use arcane terminology and disparate data formats. Deciphering payer messages requires sophisticated technology, skilled personnel, and time.

Payers also report only one error at a time. So, once you correct that error and resubmit the claim, payers get another chance for a new delay, based on a "newly discovered" error.

Next, payers frequently modify both formats and regulatory compliance rules (Correct Coding Initiative, or CCI, and local medical review policy, or LMRP). Discovering changes and implementing them in your system requires both investment and time. For instance, in January 2007, thousands of physicians discovered they were having trouble getting Medicare to pay for services billed under the codes 99303 and 99333. What were they doing wrong? Answer: Medicare deleted codes 99301–99303 from CPT in 2007, forcing the physicians to review the new 99304–99306 codes in an up-to-date CPT code book. The 99331–99333 codes were also deleted in 2007, so physicians need to review the new 99324–99328 codes.

This is just one example of a systematic strategy to reduce or delay physician payments by complicating, changing, or otherwise raising physicians' costs of claims payment processes. This way, payers confront providers with a lose-lose dilemma of expensive process maintenance on the one hand and forfeited payments on the other. A practice that ignores the changes will face increased claims underpayments and rejection rates as well as higher audit risk exposure. On the other hand, staying current with format and coding rules requires continuous and expensive billing system upgrades and frequent re-education of billing personnel.

The payer-related component of the medical billing process costs an average of 8% to 10% of a provider's collections. This component includes claim generation, scrubbing, electronic submission to payers, payment posting, denial identification, follow-up, and appeal. By complicating the process, payers increase the likelihood of failing the payment and winning the subsequent appeal process. Providers face the lose-lose choice of either expensive medical billing process upgrades or forfeiture of denied payments.

Strategy 2: Reduce Allowed Fees

Average physician reimbursement from billing Medicare and commercial payers dropped 17% in 2002–2006. From 2005 to 2006, allowed amounts (Figure 3) for E&M visits alone dropped 10% nationally, 27% in the Northeast, and 20% in the Northwest (Moore, 2007).

Figure 3. Billed, Allowed, Adjusted, and Paid Amounts

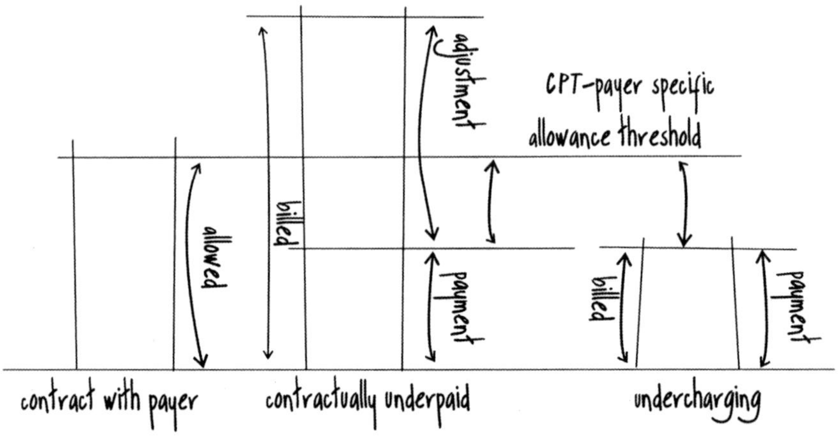

While excessive adjustment and overly conservative coding cause underpayment, providers are paid less simply by reducing allowed amounts.

Strategy 3: Increase Leverage Over Provider Through Consolidation

It is harder to drop a contract with low allowed amounts when there are fewer remaining payers. Consolidation in the insurance industry reduces competition among payers for physicians' services, allowing payers to pay less to providers. Today, 73% of the insured population are covered by just three plans; the top 10 health plans cover 106 million lives, while three plans—United, WellPoint, and Aetna—together cover 77.7 million lives. In 2006, the consolidation rate accelerated. For instance, UnitedHealthcare Group purchased 11 plans, including MetLife, PacifiCare, and Oxford (Moore, 2007). Turning down a contract offered by a payer that controls such a large portion of the population results in giving up significant revenue from medical billing.

To drive providers into networks with lower allowed amounts, payers invented the "enrollee payment program." For instance, UnitedHealthcare has announced a new national policy to discontinue direct payment of medical billing to out-of-network providers. Effective July 1, 2007, under the Pay the Enrollee program, UnitedHealthcare will direct out-of-network benefit checks to the insured member rather than nonparticipating providers. As hard as it is to collect from the insurer, surely having to chase the actual patient for payment will be harder and more costly, it will and result in even lower collections.

This policy forces the providers to choose between chasing the patients for payments or joining the payer's network. In both cases, the provider loses some earned revenue. Oxford Health Plans, a UnitedHealthcare company, implemented the Pay the Enrollee policy on April 1, 2006. According to the Oxford website announcement, Oxford may refuse to honor the assignment of benefits for claims from nonparticipating providers pursuant to language in the Certificate of Coverage. If enrollees choose to receive out-of-network treatment, the claim reimbursement may be sent directly to the enrollee. In such cases, the nonparticipating provider will be instructed to bill the covered employee for services rendered.

Additionally, effective March 1, 2007, UnitedHealthcare will fine a physician $50 if a patient goes outside the insurer's network for lab services. Physicians could also face further sanctions if patients continue to use out-of-network labs, including a "change of eligibility" in UnitedHealthcare's pay-for-performance and quality-rating programs, a "decreased fee schedule," or termination from the plan's network.

Once the provider is in the network, the payers implement profiling techniques to identify inefficient physicians. A recent Government Accountability Office (GAO) study examined 10 healthcare purchasers with profiling systems to determine whether inefficient physicians could be identified. After identifying inefficient physicians, the payers provided incentives to improve efficiency, such as the following:

- Educating physicians to encourage more efficient care
- Designating in physician directories those physicians who have met efficiency and quality standards
- Dividing physicians into tiers based on efficiency, and giving enrollees financial incentives to see physicians in their particular tiers
- Providing physicians bonuses or imposing penalties based on efficiency and quality standards
- Excluding inefficient physicians from the network

Providers face the lose-lose choice of seeing fewer patients or accepting lower rates.

Strategy 4: Underpay Claims

Partial denials cause the average medical practice to lose as much as 11% of its revenue. Denial management is difficult because of the complexity of denial causes, payer variety, and claim volume. Denial risk is not uniform across all claims. Certain classes of claims run significantly higher denial risk, depending on the claim complexity, temporary constraints, and payer idiosyncrasies:

- **Claim complexity**
  - Modifiers
  - Multiple line items

- **Temporary constraints**
  - Patient constraint (e.g., claim submission during global periods)
  - Payer constraint (e.g., claim submission timing proximity to fiscal year start)
  - Procedure constraint (e.g., experimental services)

- **Payer idiosyncrasies**
  - Bundled services
  - Disputed medical necessity

For complex claims, most payers pay the full amount for one line item but pay only a percentage of the remaining items. This payment approach creates two opportunities for underpayment: the order of paid items and the payment percentage of remaining items. Additionally, temporary constraints often cause payment errors because of the misapplication of constraints. For instance, claims submitted during the global period for services unrelated to the global period are often denied. Similar mistakes may occur at the start of the fiscal year because of the misapplication of rules for deductibles or outdated fee schedules. Payers also vary in their interpretations of CCI bundling rules or the coverage of certain services.

Strategy 5: Return for Post-Payment Audits, Demand Refunds, and Impose Penalties

The top two revenue-boosting wells for payers are drying up. Premium wars preclude insurers from raising rates, and recently enacted timely payment laws limit how long they can withhold repayment to earn interest as they had in the past. To meet profit expectations and still play within the new rules, insurers have decided to pursue the reimbursements *after* they are paid.

The Justice Department recovered a record $3.1 billion in fraud and false claims in 2006. If payer audits seem like old news to you, take another look at the numbers in Table 1. It is an undeniably unscrupulous game. And if you are a billing service provider, you should know about it, because unless you are actively working to manage audit exposure, your clients are at risk.

Table 1. Fraud Statistics			
Year	New Matters	Judgments	Average Judgment
1993	61	$155,323,165	$2,546,281
1997	347	$920,350,127	$2,652,306
2000	260	$912,388,758	$3,509,188
2003	243	$1,825,406,640	$7,511,962

If your skepticism has led you to the "rational" rebuttal that audits are expensive for everyone, rest assured that the invisible hand (gloved in technology) has helped insurers overcome this traditional obstacle. Driven by the simple goal of reducing the cost of identifying audit targets, insurers began building claims databases. With the advent of electronic submission, this became almost costless. As with many purportedly win-win propositions we've seen from insurers, electronic submission has proven to be a wolf in sheep's clothing. As providers submit claims to be paid, insurers simply add each claim to their growing database, and their computer science geeks regularly crank out reports that give executives a bird's-eye view of all their providers.

Invariably, providers are in denial about their exposure, and insurers are quick to comfort them. They will tell you that audits are an unfortunate but necessary tactic for keeping fraud in check, implying that honest providers have nothing to worry about. But insurers are not crusaders for truth and justice. Providers need to understand that **the payer's motive is money, the payer's means is a gargantuan statistical database, and every provider is an opportunity.**

Healthcare finance insiders call this a Big Brother system, and, setting aside the melodramatic implications of such a name, it's easy to see why. While executives have a soft spot for pretty charts, the true power of such a system is its ability to drill into the data and find outliers (when they talk about this type of tool, information systems specialists use jargon like data mining and online analytical processing, or OLAP). The system automatically pinpoints providers that are "easy audit targets" for one of the following reasons (see Table 2 for a short list of reports):

- They are doing something differently from the pack.
- They are lacking infrastructure for systematic denial follow-up.
- They are lacking compliant medical notes.

Table 2. Audit Triggers – Profiling Methodology	
Stage	**Report**
Prepayment Review	CCI and LMRP rules
	Inter-claim, intra-claim, cross-claim
	Lifetime duplicates
	Date range duplicates
	Re-bundling
	Modifier codes
	E&M crosswalk
	Visit level
Post-Payment Audit	Procedure repetition
	High payments per day
	Surge analysis
	Unusual modifiers
	Unusual procedure rates
	Geographic improbabilities
	5/50 patterns
External Resources	Provider watch lists
	OIG sanctions databases
	High-risk address databases

In summary, it's a fact of life: an ineffective billing system allows payers take the lead in the provider-payer tango and keep some of your practice revenue.

Chapter 4

Traditional Billing Systems

If you are like most practice owners or managers today, you use some form of the traditional billing systems that have been evolving since the birth of claim-based physician reimbursement. While these systems may use many different technologies, their underlying structures remain remarkably consistent: billing and coding personnel learn to code CMS-1500 forms, submit claims, review "scrubbing" and A/R reports, call insurers to inquire about payment status, and call providers for missing data.

If you use a traditional billing approach and find yourself frequently falling victim to the payer's system instead of your own, you have plenty of company. Here are a few reasons why:

- Traditional billing systems **limit the provider's role** in the provider-payer tango and transfer the payment and decision initiative to the payer. Except for the initial claim submission, providers are completely passive at every step (Figure 4). You wait for the payer to review the claim, wait to receive the errors, wait for the review of the corrected submission, and wait, and wait. By waiting for the payer to determine if, when, and how much of the claim will be paid, you waste valuable time and further reduce the chances of getting the claim paid.

- The average claim error rate is about 45%–55%. If your only method of finding errors is to submit the claim to the payer and wait for the payer's response, you will need multiple submission cycles for each claim until you eradicate every error.
- By delaying your own response to a billing operator's query for claim clarification, you again waste valuable time and further reduce the chances of getting the claim paid.

Figure 4. Traditional Billing Model

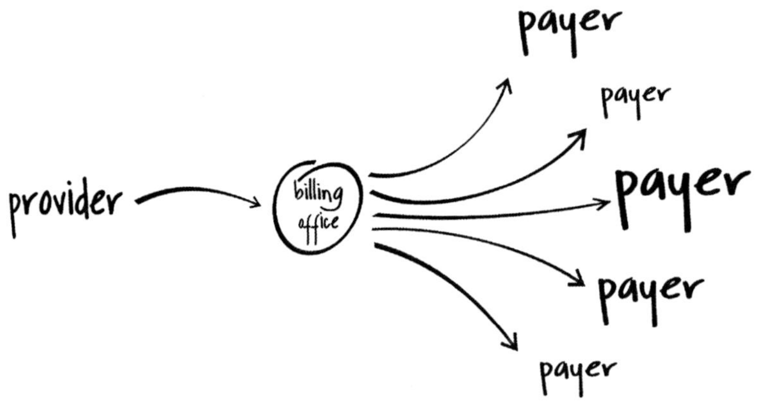

The traditional billing model confines providers to a passive role in the payer-provider tango, limited to claim submission and waiting for information from the payer.

- If your billing operator delays follow-up or selectively follows up on big-balance claims only, you may be

causing the following:
- **Encouraging** the payer to keep accumulating a significant portion of your revenue
- **Increasing your audit risk** as you signal the payer that you might not have an adequate infrastructure to properly document every patient visit, just as you are unable to discover underpayments

- If you do not manage the individual productivity of billing personnel, you create three kinds of opportunities for the payers to keep your money:
  - You deprive your billing personnel of improving their skills and productivity. You simply do not know what the person working for you has done to get the claim paid and how long each action took.
  - Without "grand error" perspective, you prevent your entire billing infrastructure from improving its performance and you are unable to keep up with the payers that frequently change formats and billing compliance requirements.
  - You encourage the billing office to simply collect fees only on uncontested and easily paid claims, forfeiting payments of problematic claims without even trying any collections effort.

Be aware that, if you follow a traditional billing system, you will fall into the payer's system and wind up doing what the payer expects—i.e., you will leave a significant part of your money with the payer.

Chapter 5

The Vericle System – A Better Way

To get the vast majority of claims paid in full and on time, you must employ a billing system that matches the power of the payer's system! The Vericle Billing System (Figure 5) is a no-nonsense approach to billing that frames the provider-payer tango as a business interaction among equals. The practice

Figure 5. The Vericle System

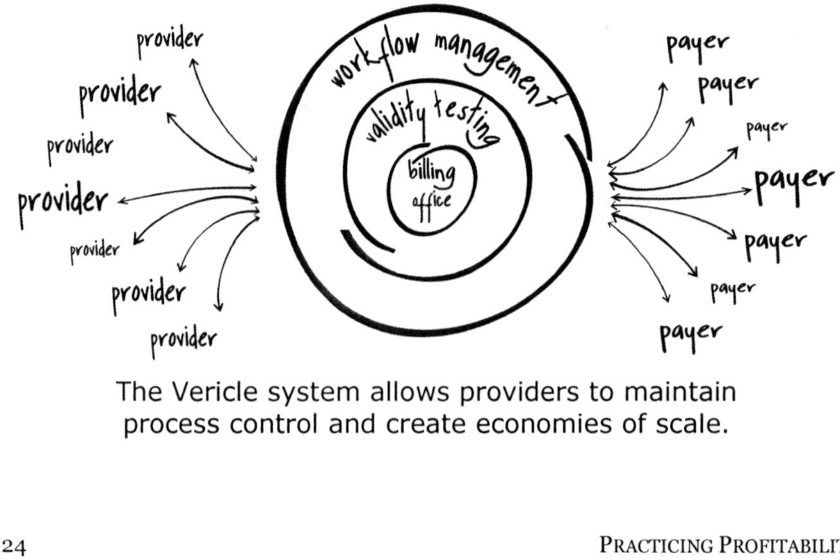

The Vericle system allows providers to maintain process control and create economies of scale.

owner and manager who uses the Vericle system gains situational control in a conflict-ridden business environment.

Instead of catching up with payers' changes and depending on favors for mission-critical payment information, you gain an accountable mechanism for getting your claims paid. The effect is based on two principles: meaningful teamwork across everybody involved in the payment process and comprehensive practice management infrastructure that matches in power the payer's infrastructure.

The Vericle Billing System is based on the following two strategies:

1. No lone provider can defeat the payer's system.
2. Match the payer's capacity with a comprehensive infrastructure.

Strategy I: No Lone Provider Can Defeat the Payer's System

The payers have allocated huge resources over the past two decades to perfect their systems. Only meaningful teamwork is effective in matching payers' methodologies to keep your money away from you. Your biller must be able to establish and maintain disciplined teamwork in two important ways:

- **Inter-provider teamwork** – Consolidate payment monitoring to accumulate the big picture of the payer's performance. Share every claims processing improvement across all providers. Enable economies of scale—the larger the network of providers using this approach, the greater and more frequent are the opportunities to get the payers to pay the money they owe you.

- **Provider-biller teamwork** – An effective and accountable communication system expedites the exchange of information and claim reprocessing. Without such a system, billers may find themselves fighting both payer and provider for missing information. Make the payment process 100% transparent to all involved. Log and communicate every action taken to get the claim paid. Establish a zero-tolerance environment for finger-pointing—we are all in the same boat.

Strategy 2: Match the Payer's Capacity with a Comprehensive Infrastructure

Your system must integrate and leverage information for four goals: payer's-side automation, audit risk management, patient relationship management, and practice workflow management.

- **Automate the payer's side of the claim flow.** Industry insiders call this connection between two different systems a "handshake." Claims stop spending time shuttling back and forth between payers and providers—so they get paid sooner and, ultimately, more often. Systems include on-demand reports to calculate reconciliations, automatically discover problematic claims, and allow continuous discovery and addition of claims processing rules to match the payer's system.

- **Reduce audit risk** – **Avoid audit threat by preparing for an audit.** Integrate disciplined visit documentation procedures using SOAP notes. Monitor and red-flag claims for audit trigger potential in real time. Track claims that might offend national or local frequencies for specific CPT codes.

- **Build patient relationships and actively maintain patient loyalty.** Focus on targeted patient attraction and loyalty development. Provide individual, timely, and meaningful information. Avoid billing confusions or errors.

- **Eliminate waste – Integrate the front and back office with a centralized practice workflow management.** Integrated scheduling and billing functionality helps avoid unbillable encounters, while integrated EMR/SOAP notes and billing helps maintain compliance, readiness for post-payment audit, and penalty avoidance. An integrated system enables automated tracking of compliance and red-flagging of audit risk.

Chapter 6

The Network Effect

Claims are not paid by waiting for the payers to pay them. Claims are paid by payers who discover that delay and underpayment are more expensive than payment in full and on time. Without a system to make the payers pay, you will default to the payer's system and find yourself giving up control.

Vericle is a system that can help make the payers pay—and it leverages the "network effect" to amplify its value. The network effect, according to Wikipedia, "causes a good or service to have a value to a potential customer which depends on the number of other customers who own the good or are users of the service." One consequence of a network effect is that the purchase of a service by one individual indirectly benefits others who also use the same service; for example, by purchasing a telephone, a person makes other telephones more useful. The resulting bandwagon effect is an example of a positive feedback loop.

For Vericle, the network effect (also known as Metcalfe's law) says that while Vericle's costs are proportional to the number of submitted claims, the value of Vericle is proportional to the square of the number of practice owners using it. For example, multiply the number of Vericle's users by 10 and your system-wide cost goes up by a factor of 10, but the value goes up a hundredfold. In other words, Metcalfe's law, as applied to Vericle, says that the value of Vericle to the individual practice owner is proportional to the number, N, of other practice owners sharing the same billing knowledge base and processes. Now multiply this value by the number of practice owners, and you have a value for the whole operation that is roughly proportional to N2 (Figure 6).

Figure 6. Vericle's Network Effect

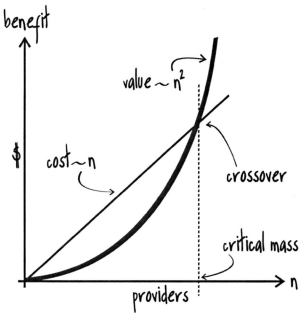

The more providers who join Vericle's network, the more benefit they receive from Vericle.

In the early 1980s, when Robert Metcalfe discovered his law, he was vague about "value." In those days, it had something to do with sharing expensive resources like fax machines and printers, exchanging electronic mail, and accessing communications technologies, such as the Internet.

For Vericle users, value is defined in four ways: improved collections, lower audit risk, efficient practice management, and added revenue sources. And, according to Metcalfe's law, this value continues to grow, long after you started using Vericle's system, in step with each newly joining practice.

Part II

Workflow Processes

If you don't know where you are going, any road will take you there.

—Cheshire Cat
Alice's Adventures in Wonderland
Lewis Carroll

Network effect becomes meaningful after reaching a certain "critical mass" of knowledge, which in turn requires a "critical mass" of practices to begin using Vericle. At the critical mass point, the value obtained from the service is greater than the price paid for it.

Four factors determine Vericle's value: efficient operations, improved collections, reduced audit risk, and added sources of revenue. Efficient operations provide value to practice owners prior to reaching critical mass.

Vericle brings efficiency using workflow technology. Workflow management technologies play two central roles in Vericle—first, for managing patient flow, and second, for billing process flow. While the two flows differ in terms of participants, expected actions, results, and exceptions, both flows capitalize on automation and exception handling.

Accordingly, this part starts with a chapter offering a clinic workflow vision for 2025. Chapter 8 introduces the concepts of Straight-Through Billing and Transparency. Chapter 9 lists criteria for evaluating billing software and office management solutions. Chapter 10 discusses profitability and the impact of office workflow on patient loyalty. Several advanced techniques for patient scheduling and appointment reminders are reviewed in Chapters 11 and 12. Chapter 13 continues to focus on billing performance by considering over-the-counter (OTC) payment problems and solutions. Centralized billing workflow and the characteristic Vericle's workbench are discussed in Chapter 14. Chapter 15 concludes this part with an advanced review of computer-aided coding concepts.

Chapter 7

Office Workflow in 2025 – Scheduling, Clinical Service, Notes, and Billing Software

Pattie Stechschulte's vision of a chiropractic office in 2025 (Stechschulte, 2003) includes simplified check-in, a complete patient checkup using noninvasive techniques, a self-configuring adjustment table that sets itself up for the next patient, a touch-screen computer system in each room loaded with intelligent software for SOAP notes, consultation modules to tap into more experienced doctors' knowledge, and a patient-friendly portal for online patient education and appointment scheduling.

While noninvasive checkups and self-configuring adjustment tables still belong to the future, the information technology aspects of Pattie's vision have already become a reality for chiropractors armed with advanced Vericle-like solutions.

First, their **patients check themselves in by swiping a key tag** in a scanner located in the front office. The key tag contains basic information about the patient (encrypted for HIPAA compliance) as well as the practice logo and phone number for a handy patient reminder. The system immediately finds the patient's SOAP notes and informs the front office person about outstanding patient balances or waiting messages.

Next, as the patient proceeds to the adjustment room, his or her SOAP notes are already displayed on a **touch-screen** computer system that the doctors have installed in each room. The system is loaded with intelligent software for care plans, SOAP notes, and retail sales products. Touch-screen technology helps doctors avoid the costly mistakes of handwritten notes. Because the note generation process is standardized, notes are complete and compliant under the scrutiny of insurance audits. Unlike a computer mouse and drop-down menus of traditional systems or the prohibitive numbers of screens in a typical PDA, touch-screen technology requires minimal eye-hand coordination; the doctor can enter information and still maintain eye contact with the patient.

Finally, as the patient leaves the office, the system **automatically generates an insurance payment claim**, presents it for the doctor's review, and immediately forwards it to the insurance company. With front-to-back office integration, advanced Vericle-like solutions deliver the claims to their destination in real time, as soon as the patient leaves the office.

Chapter 8

Straight-Through Billing

Medical billing complexity and massive volumes of daily claims render manual claims processes incapable of protecting both the provider and the payer from underpayments, overpayments, and billing compliance violations. Straight-Through Billing (STB) addresses complexity and volume processing problems by automating the majority of the claim flow and focusing the billing follow-up specialists on exceptions only. An STB process flags problems, routes them for follow-up, and enables online correction and resubmission. STB methodology implements billing service transparency and focuses management on strategic process improvement opportunities.

Straight-Through Billing integrates the billing process into the practice management workflow, automates the vast majority of transactions, focuses manual labor on exceptions, and establishes a process for continuous improvement.

First, integrated practice management and billing workflow connects patient scheduling, medical record management, and billing into a single flow. Every participant of the practice management workflow receives a unified and coherent picture of practice workload, patient and provider location, resource availability, and cash flow.

Next, transaction automation streamlines and expedites the billing process by automating claim validation, payer message reconciliation, and billing workflow management:

- Automated claim validation eliminates errors downstream and reduces processing time because it flags errors before submitting the claim to the payer.
- Automated claim message reconciliation eliminates the costly search for the original claim and standardizes message communication, further eliminating the need to decipher the (often cryptic) payer's message.
- Automated billing workflow management drives the follow-up discipline required for the resolution of claim denial and underpayment incidents, and it establishes a high degree of process transparency for all billing process participants, resulting in full and timely payments.

Third, focusing manual labor on exceptions requires timely exception identification, routing to follow-up personnel, online error correction, and rigorous follow-up tracking. Again, process transparency, as implemented in Vericle-like systems, enables tracking exception follow-up.

Finally, a process for continuous improvement requires continuous observability of every process attribute and a modification methodology for both automated claim processing and manual exception follow-up tracking.

Straight-Through Billing implements billing transparency by design because billing transparency is an integral attribute of every component of the STB process.

Straight-Through Billing Architecture

The Straight-Through Billing systems architecture mirrors the architecture of general Straight-Through Processing (STP) systems developed for the financial services industry. Such systems require effective workflow management, a knowledge-based validation system, connectivity to all process participants (including online data reconciliation), and tracking of problem resolution. Therefore, a typical Vericle-like STB system has a three-tiered architecture:

- Back-end processing engine designed for a high-volume transaction processing environment
- Middle tier using Java Servlet technology
- Front end using an HTML-JavaScript, zero-footprint client

An STB system (e.g., Vericle) following the methodology outlined above implements rich functionality, which allows the following to be automated:

- Computer-aided preferential patient scheduling
- Integrated electronic medical records
- Online computer-aided coding
- Real-time claim validation and patient eligibility testing
- Electronic claim submission
- Payment posting, reconciliation, and verification of meeting contractual obligations
- Monitoring of audit risk and billing compliance
- Tracking of denial appeal process

Quantitative STB Management

Straight-Through Billing methodology allows for quantitative management, since the likelihood of failure of the entire process can be estimated as the product of such items for each individual workflow step. A Vericle-like STB system tracks the percentage of clean claims (claims paid in full, and within the allocated time frame, without any manual intervention) and focuses the management on those process aspects that yield the greatest potential improvement. Thus, STB methodology focuses on exceptions both at the tactical and strategic management levels.

Chapter 9

Practice Perfect – Ten Criteria for the Best Billing Software and Office Management Solution

" Information Technology (IT) is a necessary component of a modern chiropractic office," says Dr. Greg Loman of Trinity Chiropractic and Maximized Living Inc. "IT helps maintain patient relationships, control audit risks, and ensure full and timely billing."

Dr. Loman has established one of the most successful chiropractic offices in the world, seeing over 60,000 patients a year. A world power boat racing champion, Dr. Loman has learned what it takes to be the very best.

Maximized Living—which he co-founded with Dr. Ben Lerner, author of *Body by God*, *Generation XL*, and *One-Minute Wellness*—helps chiropractors and students across the world. Their clients have the largest, most successful clinics in the profession today.

"Complete practice workflow solution starts with appointment scheduling and includes SOAP notes and billing," says Dr.

Brian Capra, who used to work with Drs. Lerner and Loman. "Few vendors today offer such integrated packages as they require powerful technologies used by trained and skilled personnel implementing rigorous and disciplined service processes."

Chiropractic IT must meet five functional criteria and five technology criteria:

1. **Clinical Relevance** – Technology can only help the healing process if it helps make treatment decisions at the point of care. Therefore, it must be available next to the treatment table, and it must have an intuitive user interface to facilitate simple data entry and help online reporting.

2. **Patient Relationship Management** – Successful practice development requires perfectly managed patient relationships, starting with establishing and tracking financial care plans, appointment reminders, and balance follow-ups and avoiding unbillable appointments.

3. **Compliant SOAP Notes** – SOAP is short for Subjective, Objective, Assessment, and Plan:
   • **Subjective** describes the patient's current condition, including all pertinent and negative symptoms. Document how symptoms impact activities of daily living. Use the standard SOAP format, modified to SOAAP by adding an extra "A" for Activities of Daily Living.
   • **Objective** includes vital signs, findings from physical examinations, and results from laboratory tests. Document functional measure-

ments (e.g., range of motion), comparison data, test results, co-morbidities, etc., to paint a picture of what is going on with the patient.

- **Assessment** is a quick summary of the patient with the main symptoms and diagnosis, including a differential diagnosis, a list of other possible diagnoses (usually in the order of most likely to least likely).
- **Plan** is what the healthcare provider will do to treat the patient's concerns. This should address each item of the differential diagnosis. Document goals for the patient, and establish a reasonable timeline to reach those goals. Update your treatment plan every 30 days or 12 visits or any time there is a significant change in the patient's condition (e.g., exacerbation, new injury, discharge exam). Document the patient's progress toward those goals in the daily SOAAP notes.

4. **Full and Timely Payments** – Revenue-cycle management software must help the practice manager to make sure that every service encounter gets paid in full and on time. It must provide a full and detailed 24/7 account of all actions on every claim, systematic discovery of denials, patient invoicing, electronic claims submissions to payers, payment posting and reconciliation with charges, HIPAA compliance, built-in tests for medical necessity, and comprehensive online reporting.

5. **Audit Risk Management** – Audit risk management

consists of continuous monitoring for potential compliance violations and meticulous management of patient encounter notes.

6. **Reporting and Transparency** – Without transparency, billing may not be reliable. To be able to observe every step of the billing process on a continuous 24/7 basis, reporting must be available using a secure HIPAA-compliant connection over the Internet. Vendors that manage their own billing technology typically have better control of reporting capabilities in terms of scope, analysis, frequency, and transparency. At the minimum, the following features must be available:

   - **Operational Report** – Showing total claims and dollar amounts submitted, paid, adjusted, written off, and failed. It allows breakdown by CPT, payer, referral, or a combination of such dimensions.
   - **Denials Report** – Showing the list of denied claims and a log of follow-up actions. If you sort it by amount paid, you can determine the smallest payment that the billing service will fight for.
   - **Compliance Report** – Showing the potential for post-payment audit and itemizing compliance violations.

   Reports must allow arbitrary data aggregation and drill-in. Exporting to Excel spreadsheets for further analysis is a very useful feature.

7. **Billing Quality Metric** – Make a list of metrics

available online. Focus on collections completeness and payment delay. Can the system report the differences between payers and between various CPT codes in real time? What is the denial follow-up success rate?

8. **Data Entry Protocols** – Modern technologies allow the doctor to take over coding and reduce the billing role to claims processing and follow-up. A technology-competent vendor will supply your "superbill" online, along with a separate form for patient and charge entry, EOB posting, and online claim editing. Similarly, much of data entry validity, including some claim scrubbing, will be done online at the point of data entry.

9. **ASP or SaaS Delivery Model** – Rapid technology progress results in a low return on investment in software licenses, typical of client-server technology. Therefore, monthly leasing arrangements with zero up-front investment, typical of ASP (application service provider) or SaaS (Software as a Service) delivery models are preferable to license purchase.

10. **Data Security and Protection** – Review data center facilities. Ask for evidence on HIPAA compliance; claims must be viewed only on a "need to know" basis, and access to claims and modifications must be thoroughly documented. Data must be protected with redundant disaster recovery measures. Review backup processes, backup intervals, and data restore capabilities.

Summary

Increasing regulatory scrutiny, poor in-house billing performance, and rapid technology progress are key growth drivers in chiropractic information technology. On one hand, thousands of outsourced billing solutions and software vendors ensure continued competitiveness in terms of both service quality and pricing. On the other hand, the lack of standards and uniform metrics among the vendors, combined with their large numbers, frustrates the selection process. Ten effective guidelines will streamline your outsourced solution selection process and reduce the costs of switching vendors.

Chapter 10

Patient Loyalty and Profitability

Patient loyalty is a key to continued practice success in terms of both recurring and new revenue. As patients keep returning to your practice, it maintains revenue stability—and as patients refer their friends and family, your practice billing collections grow. In terms of profitability, new patient acquisition is, by an order of magnitude, more expensive than loyalty maintenance for existing patients.

Time delay is a major problem of eroding patient loyalty. By the time you discover that you have a patient loyalty problem, it is typically too late to do anything about the patients who have already left. Patients typically desert you without saying "good-bye," and your only way to discover patient attrition is by observing lower collections and more free time on your appointment scheduler.

Frequent patient communication is the only effective way to reduce such a time delay and increase the likelihood of timely loyalty problem identification and resolution. Such patient communications can revolve around any of the practice management components—from patient scheduling to SOAP notes to special healthcare literature to medical billing, insurance payments, co-pays, and deductibles.

Patient Identification for Targeted Communications

It's convenient to view targeted communications from the patient visit perspective:

- Patients due for scheduled appointments or who owe you payments need a reminder.
- Patients who recently had an appointment need results, interpretation, prescriptions, and follow-up.
- Patients with prescriptions that are about to expire may need to schedule a visit.
- Patients who have not had an appointment for a long time need a reminder to schedule a checkup. A screening procedure schedule should be generated using specific combinations of procedure (CPT) and diagnosis (ICD) codes.
- Patients with chronic conditions or permanent injuries need literature about recent progress in treating their conditions.
- Patients who have had a long series of appointments need progress reports.
- Patients who receive good progress reports need to be solicited for referrals.
- Patients with bad progress reports need special literature and special appointments.
- Patients waiting in the reception area need access to customized information about their specific conditions.

To generate such lists of patients, your systems must combine scheduling, medical notes, and billing data in a single database.

Patient Communications Venue

While traditional phone and conventional mail systems are still in use, the Internet is the most obvious choice for communicating with patients. A custom, HIPAA-compliant patient portal is the least expensive way to allow your patients to interact with you outside the clinic at their convenience and privacy. Patients can do the following:

- Review reminders and schedule appointments
- Review visit results
- Ask you clarifying questions
- Request prescriptions
- Read special literature and progress reports that you send them
- Send you referrals
- Review medical bills and pay invoices
- Track their medical costs

Active patient loyalty management, based on selective patient identification for targeted communications at the patient's convenience, is one of the most effective ways to improve practice profitability.

Chapter 11

Computer-aided Patient Scheduling

Without a computerized scheduler, a practice has a less than 2% chance to earn the title of a "better performing practice," according to the Medical Group Management Association (MGMA). A massive investment in scheduling features across a wide spectrum of billing products is another indication of the importance of computerized scheduling; during May and June of 2006, Billing Wiki (www.billingwiki.com) cited 26 software products that offer some aspect of patient scheduling.

Convenience and front office efficiencies are two obvious benefits of a computerized scheduling system, since without it, the only manual way to find out if a specific patient has a scheduled appointment is to flip through the appointment book page by page. Worse, manual scheduling hurts both patient satisfaction and practice financial performance because of scheduling inconsistencies and unbilled (and therefore unpaid) visits.

But the benefits of integrated computerized scheduling stretch far beyond convenience, front office efficiencies, and better charge follow-up of stand-alone, albeit computerized, scheduling. A well-designed and integrated scheduler allows preferential patient scheduling, which, along with improved controls, helps revenue optimization and practice compliance. Below, we review key aspects of computerized scheduling, and we demonstrate important benefits of integrated scheduling, billing, and compliance management.

Scheduling Policies

Computerized schedulers allow a combination of single- or multiple-interval scheduling, with open-access scheduling subject to various priority constraints. Such priority constraint-driven, open-access scheduling creates preferential appointments based on patient demographics or insurance coverage.

Single-interval scheduling allocates appointments at regular intervals—every 5 to 15 minutes, depending on the specialty. The downside of single-interval scheduling is that as soon as one appointment takes longer than the allocated slot, all subsequent patients have to wait.

Multiple-interval scheduling also sets appointments at regular intervals—however, unlike single-interval scheduling, it allocates the length of the appointment depending on the chief complaint. Such scheduling requires up-front categorization of key appointment types and their projected lengths. For instance, an initial appointment might take 30 minutes, while a routine injection might take only 5 minutes.

Open-access scheduling requires holding open several appointments every day. These open appointments are filled only within 48 hours of the appointment, catering to same-day or last-minute patient requests. Open-access scheduling improves access to the physician, reduces no-shows, and eliminates patient screening time. The downside of open-access scheduling is, of course, the potential for longer patient waiting lines or physician idle time because of the inability to maintain a predictable patient flow.

One way to balance practice workload is to schedule group, routine, or repeat appointments during slow hours. For instance, pediatric well-child visits or patients with a particular chronic disease—such as congestive heart failure or diabetes—could be scheduled for early mornings, when there are typically fewer patients waiting in line. These scheduled visits include educational components and often involve multidisciplinary teams. Patients also benefit from the socialization aspect of group visits, as members encourage one another, exercise together, and so forth. A good scheduler will allow a repeat appointment schedule subject to total frequency and time slot constraints.

Compliance Process

An integrated scheduler verifies the filing of a signed patient consent form—and, in certain cases, a signed ABN form. An ABN (Advance Beneficiary Notice) serves three goals:

- To protect the beneficiaries from liability for services denied as not reasonable (depends on the frequency or duration) and necessary (depends on the diagnosis and the provider's specialty)
- To protect the provider's revenue by shifting financial liability for denied services to the patient
- To provide documentation for a Medicare audit

For more complex procedures, the scheduler warns the front office about the need to obtain up front all of the required diagnostic test results and clearances.

Billing Interface

The integrated scheduler avoids unbillable patient encounters and reconciles visits with patient balances. It checks outstanding patient balances and verifies coverage and eligibility at the point of scheduling, prior to the appointment. In many cases, such a test discovers data entry errors too, reducing the payment cycle at later stages.

Additionally, the insurance company may require referrals or separate pre-authorization/certification for certain procedures, refusing the payment if the procedure was performed without a referral or pre-authorization. The integrated scheduler has access to medical records to supply necessary background and diagnosis information to obtain pre-authorization. Finally, without the ability to reconcile visits with payments, the practice owner cannot be sure that every visit resulted in a payment.

Practice Flow Interface

The integrated scheduler manages the entire patient flow, providing continuously updated arrival lists, checkoffs, and office/room tracking. Further, the scheduler tracks no-shows and follow-up actions. Detailed reports include daily schedules, load reports, missed appointments, free time, canceled appointments, etc.

Patient Interface

Advanced schedulers include appointment reminders and provide online registration and online scheduling request forms. Online scheduling request forms must take into account the risk of scheduling patients beyond the scope of the practice, which a live operator would have screened out.

Summary

Traditional stand-alone scheduling systems reduce idle time for employees, lower provider frustration, and reduce patient waiting time. Modern integrated schedulers accomplish more ambitious goals of increasing revenue, reducing administrative costs, and shortening billing cycles. An integrated scheduler handles multiple providers, locations, scheduling policies, and patient preparation processes, and it has bi-directional compliance and billing interfaces. Most importantly, an integrated scheduler implements a consistent preferential scheduling policy.

Chapter 12

Appointment Reminders for Revenue Protection and Patient Relationship Management

When patients miss appointments, they interrupt the flow of patient care, impede clinic productivity, and signal an eroding patient loyalty. The rate of no-shows runs at 30% for the average family practice. A missed appointment amounts to missed billing revenue. Worse, if the clinicians are part-time or full-time staff rather than contracted, they sit idle on the company clock, losing money with each passing minute. Finally, a missed appointment could be a symptom of a deserting patient, signaling a potential loss of long-term billing revenue.

Reminder calls for upcoming appointments and follow-up calls on recent no-shows are effective strategies for billing revenue protection because they reduce the number of no-shows and help early identification of incipient patient attrition and other patient relationship problems. Vendors of reminder call services quote no-show reduction rates of 50% (Hashim, Franks, & Fiscella, 2001). They also mention comparable improvement of long-term patient loyalty. Other no-show reduction strategy components include charges for missed appointments, no-show statistics analysis, and overbooking.

While recognizing the benefits of reminder calls, busy practice owners often neglect or postpone reminder and follow-up calls because of other office management priorities, such as personnel issues or billing. As with any other management initiative, to get results, a reminder call strategy must be implemented systematically and consistently.

Reminder call automation delivers the benefits of billing revenue protection and patient relationship management in a disciplined and systematic fashion and at a significantly lower cost. Successful implementation of reminder call automation depends on technology and requires the following components:

1. **Flexible messaging** – A successful appointment reminder to consistently fit the culture of your practice, location, and specific appointment type. Typically, a practice uses new patient, existing patient, and recall patient messages as well as several specialty messages.

2. **Appointment scheduler integration** – A seamless method for retrieving the appointment information without involving the medical staff. Ideally, the message scheduler should be integrated within electronic medical billing software, providing transparent access to both the patient appointment scheduler and patient financial records.

3. **Call scheduling** – The ability to schedule and automatically call patients with a personalized human

voice message.

4. **High-quality infrastructure** – A facility with the highest-quality fiberoptic feed, digital lines allowing unsurpassed message quality, and call progress detection accuracy. This technology helps to do the following:

   a. Avoid the pause that accompanies most automated messages. In fact, any pause after the first sound could lead a patient to hang up or lead to improper call diagnosis.
   b. Use call progress detection to determine if the phone was answered by a person or by an answering machine. This can mean the difference between leaving a complete message or only a short segment of the message on the answering machine.

Finally, when shopping for automated reminder services, focus on vendors that offer SaaS-driven service and pricing. "Software as a Service" vendors of reminder call automation solutions price their services for only the calls they make, while you avoid purchasing hardware/software and associated management and maintenance costs. In financial management terms, the SaaS proposition is equivalent to turning capital expense into operating expense, which translates into a better balance sheet and lower risk.

Chapter 13

Over-the-Counter Payment Performance

For many practices, the proportion of over-the-counter (OTC) payments has recently grown from an average of 15% to as high as 75% of total payments. Systematic OTC collections, including a measurable process that emphasizes up-front collections, often yield double-digit billing performance improvement. Most importantly, a disciplined and transparent collections process improves provider-patient communications, while early payment collections are also quicker and easier. Better communications and happier patients mean better health and a more profitable practice.

OTC payments include co-pays, fees for noncovered elective services or retail products, and any outstanding balances. Successful collections of OTC payments require a measurable collections process, a specialized information technology infrastructure, and adequate personnel training and discipline.

OTC payment collection performance and costs greatly depend on the elapsed time between service and payment. The dependence of collection performance on timing stems from the dynamic nature of the price-value relation. Initially, perception of value received is high in the patient's mind. Similarly, the correlation between value and price is also high. However, OTC payment collections grow more difficult in step with the fading memory of the service's benefit.

Systematic measurement of OTC payment quality is critical for its performance improvement. Vericle's OTC payment quality metrics include the percentage of accounts receivable beyond 120 days and the time spent on collecting on old account balances. While the national average of the first metric hovers around 18%, some practices have accumulated as much as 50% of their accounts receivable beyond 120 days. The second metric measures the front office collections efficiency, and it too varies widely between a few hours per month and double-digit hours per week spent by front office personnel chasing unpaid OTC invoices.

According to Vericle experience, the following systematic and measurable payment collections process leverages electronic medical billing software and establishes the discipline required for double-digit billing collections improvement:

1. **Publish your payment collections policy** and standard responses to typical patient objections.

2. **Clarify patient statements** generated by your electronic medical billing software.
   a. Make outstanding balances easily identifiable.
   b. Add specific language about the time period expected for payment of the balance due (typically upon service or product delivery).
   c. Include a phone number for patients to call with questions.

3. **Use electronic medical billing software** to do the

following:

    a. Test a patient's eligibility and coverage (the results of such a test define a patient's co-pay prior to arrival at the clinic).

    b. Generate front office alerts about an impending visit by a patient with an unpaid OTC balance.

4. **Train clinic physicians** to direct patients to front office staff to review financial statements.

5. **Train your front office** to collect OTC payments.

    a. Hold your front office staff accountable by setting up specific and personal collection goals.

    b. Use electronic medical billing software to track collections performance by individual front office staff.

    c. Establish personal awards for accomplishing collections goals, and periodically review personal collections performance.

    d. Train your office staff to receive electronic medical billing software alerts.

    e. Develop a payment collections script and rehearse it with front office staff to improve staff-patient communications.

Summary

Successful OTC payment collections help patient relationship management and improve practice profitability. They require a measurable collections process, a specialized information technology infrastructure, and adequate personnel training and discipline.

Chapter 14

Centralized Billing Workflow

Reducing accounts receivable is a key responsibility of the billing function in a medical practice. This chapter compares traditional (distributed) billing functions with centralized workflow management. It shows that centralized workflow management yields significant advantages over the distributed approach in terms of the ability to manage accounts receivable. However, it also requires significant investments in process, technology, and personnel training.

Benefits

Centralized workflow management is superior to traditional billing operations management because it enables continuous billing process improvements and helps avoid the repetition of errors while reducing the dependency on specific individual billing knowledge. The billing process improves systematically along the key performance dimensions, including the amount and timeliness of the payment.

Centralized workflow management accomplishes such important benefits using a two-pronged approach that's based on formal encoding of billing and compliance knowledge and on a computer program to apply the knowledge and manage claim follow-up lists.

As an encoded billing knowledge base grows, the accuracy of the claims and the speed of the process increases. Additionally, the staff can spend more time focusing on exceptions, while an increasing majority of claims are processed automatically.

Moreover, a centralized workflow shares its billing rules across all providers and billers. Therefore, errors discovered and corrected for one provider will be avoided in the future for all of the providers using the system.

Workflow

Workflow is defined as a sequence of actions performed on a claim until it is paid. Centralized workflow management must quickly separate "clean" claims from potential failures, submit clean claims to payers, and flag potential failures for correction. Workflow must also track the correction process, ensuring its integration with other sources of failures and its successful completion. Finally, workflow must facilitate meticulous documentation of every step to enable continuous improvement and learning from experience.

Failed Claim

A failed claim is a claim that is flagged by the workflow system up front as an invalid claim, is rejected by the payer after submission, or is not properly adjudicated within 30 days—in other words, a claim that requires follow-up.

Workbench

Centralized workflow manages such follow-up lists of failed claims using workbenches. A workbench is a list of failed claims assigned to an individual biller or operator. Such an individual assignment of work enables continuous and individual performance tracking and improvement.

Activity Triggers

In a medical billing operation, the follow-up lists and to-do lists of individual actions for each failed claim constantly change. To manage multiple to-do lists, the centralized workflow system has activity triggers. Activity triggers are the heart of task automation; they help determine what's important. Activity triggers match up promises with events and manage individual work queues in the process.

In order to remember to call a payer or provider weeks after the phone conversation in which a payment or claim clarification was promised, a billing clerk must sort through a call-on-receipt folder several times a day. Activity triggers eliminate the reliance on personal memory and enable communication between individual workbenches. They are the strings that tie billing activities together. For example, when Mary from the provider's office updates the claim with the correct ICD-9, the system needs to be aware that the claim is ready for validation—and John in the billing office needs to know so he can review it again to see if the validation failed or to schedule its transmission to the payer.

Task Automation

Centralized workflow eliminates paper-based steps. Like a relay team passing the baton, the billing staff members electronically pass along their work without delays. Instead of printing, faxing, and following up with an email or a phone call, all tasks arrive complete with supporting documentation. Rather than thumbing through reams of paper and reading scribbled notes, billers receive on-screen reminders when tasks are due.

Process Monitoring

Centralized workflow also simplifies process monitoring. Providers and managers use dashboards to review key indicators. Like activity triggers, dashboards help focus personnel on what is important from a high-level perspective. They show key business information that tells us if we are paid more or less over time, if our charges are going up or down, and if our follow-up policies are too lenient. They tell us whether we are heading in the right direction and act like lighthouses to keep us off the shoals. When we see that warning light, we can drill into the details and take corrective action.

Summary

The key difference between Vericle-like centralized workflow management and traditional approaches is that a centralized workflow guides the operator to identify claims that need follow-up. There is no need to manually look up reports to analyze data and select claims for follow-up. A Vericle-like approach ensures follow-up consistency and timeliness.

Chapter 15

Computer-aided Coding

The average practice submits half of its codes wrong, while some practices rarely exceed more than one correct code out of every five. Inexact and inconsistent coding increases the risks of undercharging, overcharging, and post-payment audit. This chapter outlines the evolution of coding from an individualistic art toward a disciplined and systematic process.

It is convenient to review the role of coding in the context of the entire claim processing cycle: patient appointment scheduling, pre-authorization, patient encounter note creation, charge generation, claim scrubbing, claim submission to payer, and follow-up, which in turn includes denial or underpayment identification, payment reconciliation, and appeal management. The importance of thorough knowledge and the correct application of coding rules at the charge generation stage of the claim processing cycle are well known and have been frequently discussed. Less obvious, but no less important, is the ability to make correct interpretations of the same rules at the claim follow-up stage during denial or underpayment analysis and upon receiving the payment and explanation of benefits.

Coding is difficult because of a four-dimensional complexity. First, the sheer volume and intricacy of coding rules makes it difficult to select the right procedure code, correct modifier, and necessary diagnosis code for the given medical note. For instance, a claim will get denied if you charged for two CPT codes but provided an ICD-9 code that shows medical necessity for only one CPT code. Next, the payer-specific modifications exacerbate the complexity of coding, creating the need to code or process differently the same procedures, depending on the payer. For example, some payers require medical notes attached to some CPT codes in addition to standard ICD-9 codes. Third, the codes and regulations change over time, necessitating continuous coding education and re-education. Finally, charge generation and claim follow-up are disconnected in space and time, and they're often performed by different people, adding to the confusion and costs of the claim processing cycle.

Only experienced coders can handle such complexity, but experience too often turns into a handicap—for example, in the absence of a reliable self-correcting process, the coder or the follow-up person may make the same mistake over and over. Hence, ad hoc coding is error-prone and expensive. Paper superbill-driven coding improves upon traditional coding because it allows fewer errors and eliminates some of the costs. Computer-aided coding with an integrated superbill completes the transformation of coding from an individualistic art toward a disciplined and systematic process, and it is the most reliable and least expensive solution.

Traditional Coding

Since the practice owner is ultimately responsible for coding quality, it behooves the physician to personally manage the coding process. But traditionally, in the absence of systematic practice management, the physician looked for a coding approach to avoid the burden of coding. Such an approach to coding is both error-prone and expensive. The average error rate for CPT coding is 45%–55% (Healthcare Financial Management Association, 2003) (Figure 7). Some specialties (e.g., interventional radiologists) have trouble exceeding even 18% of correct coding (Healthcare Financial Management Association).

Figure 7. Billing Error Distribution

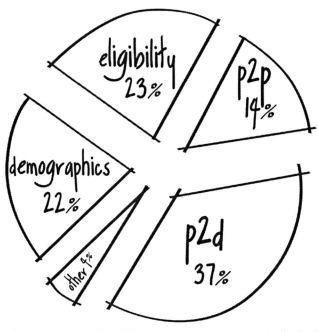

Medical necessity (Procedure to Diagnosis "P2D"
and Procedure to Procedure "P2P")
make up more than half of the errors.

Traditional coding involves the doctor, data entry personnel, and a certified coder. The doctor dictates, types, or handwrites descriptions of diagnoses and procedures, without listing actual codes. The data entry personnel enter codes based on reading the doctor's descriptions, and the certified coder supervises and audits the quality of coding by the data entry personnel.

The traditional coding process is error-prone because the certified coder does not audit 100% of entered codes and because such a process does not have a vehicle for context maintenance between the charge's creation and the claim's follow-up stages. The errors may become especially expensive upon post-payment audit of the charges by the insurance company. This process is also expensive because multiple people are involved in the coding process and because the errors, if discovered at all, will be discovered only downstream, raising the costs of error correction.

Paper Superbill-driven Coding

A pre-compiled, superbill-driven coding process places the doctor in control of coding, ties together claim creation and follow-up stages, and avoids many shortcomings of traditional coding. Such a process delivers the twofold advantage of lower cost and improved communication. First, the doctor personally codes at the end of the patient encounter without involving data entry personnel in the middle. Second, the paper superbill serves as a formal vehicle for coding information communication between the charge creation and claim follow-up stages. Additionally, a pre-compiled superbill improves coding consistency across all doctors within the same practice.

This superbill creation process has four stages:

1. List the codes used most often first (use a CPT frequency report for discovery)
2. List the diagnosis codes

3. Leave room for ancillary services
4. Include the patient's information

Along with the advantages over the traditional coding process, the paper-based superbill still has four shortcomings. First, the data must be re-entered into the system from the paper superbill, introducing the potential for errors. Next, the superbill must be reviewed periodically to adjust for changes in practice operations. Worse, it is difficult to keep up with changes in coding regulations, necessary modifiers, and bundling decisions that differ across various payers. Finally, the paper superbill contributes nothing to up-front coding error identification and correction, which can delay potential error identification and resolution to post-submission or, even worse, to post-payment phases. Obviously, the later in the process the error is identified, the more expensive is its correction.

Computer-aided Coding with Integrated Superbill

Computerization and integration overcome most of the problems of paper superbills. They eliminate duplicate data entry; automate code review and adjustment for frequency, practice operations, and payer idiosyncrasies; and shift much of the error identification and correction from the post-payment stage to the claim pre-submission stage.

Computer-aided coding with an integrated superbill offers multiple advantages:

1. **Dynamic** – Adjusts for changes in practice operations and payer specifics. For instance, it adds an automated alert to satisfy unique payer demands, such as requests for paid drug invoices in addition to an in-

jection CPT code and J code for supplies.

2. **Precise** – Matches codes to EMR, and alerts in real time about potential coding errors—such as confusing modifiers 59, 76, 77, and 91 for repeat procedure or test, or not coding the ICD-9 code to the highest level of possible digits in spite of a specific diagnostic available in EMR.

3. **Defensive** – Allows for real-time profiling of coding patterns to alert about potential audit flags.

4. **Reliable** – Facilitates end-of-day juxtaposition of visits with charges, avoiding unpaid visits.

5. **Inexpensive** – Eliminates the extra data entry step and associated costs, because the doctor can use it directly.

Summary

Coding is a mission-critical responsibility of the practice owner. Computer-aided coding with an integrated superbill places the doctor in control and enables a dynamic, precise, reliable, consistent, defensive, and inexpensive coding process. Superbill digitization and integration overcome the four-dimensional coding complexity; tie it to EMR, patient scheduling, and billing (i.e., to the entire spectrum of practice management functions), and require powerful Vericle-like computing platforms.

Part III

Electronic Medical Records, SOAP Notes, and Care Plans

The adventures first . . . explanations take such a dreadful time.

> —The Gryphon
> *Alice's Adventures in Wonderland*
> Lewis Carroll

Well-managed medical records and SOAP notes bring two key values to both patients and practice owners: better healthcare and lower audit risk. A solid note management discipline is entirely dependent on internal practice management processes. Therefore, EMR and SOAP notes belong to a "pre-network effect" service category, designed to deliver value to practice owners independently of the number of practices using the Vericle network. Efficiency then becomes the key challenge of EMR and SOAP notes—but what is the best way to implement them to deliver their values most efficiently, without adding costs?

This part contains five chapters about EMR and SOAP notes. Chapter 16 outlines requirements for intelligent notes. Chapter 17 presents the challenges and solutions for integration of best-of-breed EMR and billing technologies. Chapter 18 discusses physician interface issues in EMR and billing systems and presents five ways to resolve them. A construction methodology for a result-driven and compliant care plan is presented in Chapter 19.

Chapter 16

Intelligent SOAP Notes

Doctors and therapists must produce clinical documentation in ever-increasing volumes and detail to ensure the best healthcare, get medical claims paid in full and on time, and protect the practice from post-payment audits and unfair litigation.

But the speed of completing visit documentation conflicts with documentation accuracy and thoroughness. For insurance companies, patient visit documentation must be precise and comprehensive. If the quality of documentation is high, the medical billing appeals on unpaid claims are paid faster and at a higher rate. Otherwise, appeals are denied and the practice becomes vulnerable to post-payment audits, refunds, and penalties.

Insurance companies do not care how long it takes to produce good documentation. But for the provider, slow documentation impedes practice profitability and wastes valuable time. The doctor must be done with visit documentation by the time the patient leaves the office.

To ensure comprehensive note coverage, the healthcare industry adopted a two-pronged, structured approach. First, the doctor uses the SOAP notes format, which reflects four key stages of patient care—Subjective observations, Objective symptoms, diagnostic Assessment, and the treatment Plan:

1. **Subjective** – The initial portion of the SOAP note format consists of subjective observations. These are symptoms typically expressed verbally by the patient. They include the patient's descriptions of pain or discomfort, the presence of nausea or dizziness, or other descriptions of dysfunction.

2. **Objective** – The next part of the format includes symptoms that can be actually measured, seen, heard, touched, felt, or smelled. Included in objective observations are vital signs such as temperature, pulse, respiration, skin color, swelling, and the results of diagnostic tests.

3. **Assessment** – Assessment is the diagnosis of the patient's condition based on subjective observations and objective symptoms. In some cases, the diagnosis may be a simple determination, while in other cases, it may include multiple diagnosis possibilities.

4. **Plan** – The last part of the SOAP note is the treatment plan, which may include laboratory and/or radiological tests ordered for the patient, medications ordered, treatments performed (e.g., minor surgical procedure), patient referrals (sending the patient to a specialist), patient disposition (e.g., home care, bed rest, short-term or long-term disability, days excused from work, admission to the hospital), and patient directions and follow-up directions for the patient.

Next, each one of the four key SOAP stages consists of templates reflecting multiple possibilities for each stage. Templates, organized according to SOAP order, ensure comprehensive coverage and allow the doctor to simply check multiple selection boxes on a screen that's driven by a computer program.

Templates have attracted twofold criticism, from both the provider and the payer sides. The providers dislike the lack of built-in intelligence to reflect an individual doctor's preferences to treat patients. The payers often suspect template-generated notes of low quality and poor reflection of a patient's true state and treatment progress, because of a template's susceptibility to mechanical clicking and difficulty of interpretation.

The challenge is to combine the advantages of template and verbose formats and avoid their shortcomings to describe precise patient conditions, ensure productive medical billing, prepare for regulatory scrutiny, and improve practice productivity. To overcome the perception of mechanically generated notes while saving the doctor the time to type, some vendors have created specialized products that use randomized wording for each template. Such automatically generated notes include sentence structures that closely resemble natural speech patterns.

Flexibility and integration must be key design features of SOAP notes. In the opening section, for example, you create new patient files that grow organically with each visit or treatment. Built-in intelligence allows you to customize a document to your own preferences and observe the entire patient progress history in a single screen. Native system integration with medical billing systems enable automated claim generation, validation, and submission to payers for payment.

SOAP notes must not merely emulate the paper folder that every doctor has for every patient. They must use computer technology to help automate routine tasks and create a faster, easier, and error-free process to increase practice profitability and reduce audit risks.

Chapter 17

Best-of-Breed Billing Plus EMR –
Transition Challenges and Integration Plan

The limited choice between mediocre full-scope products and excellent single-function systems has been expanding in step with the increasing reliability of Internet technology and standardization of system interfaces.

"An integrated best-of-breed product helps patient care and clinical error reduction, financial performance, and regulatory compliance," says Boris Petrikovsky, MD, PhD, chairman of the Department of Obstetrics & Gynecology at Nassau University Medical Center and professor of Obstetrics, Gynecology, and Reproductive Medicine at Stony Brook University School of Medicine.

Comprehensive, integrated best-of-breed solutions that combine modern EMR software and billing service can be utilized under the "pay as you go" business model. The SaaS (Software as a Service) model allows physicians to confirm the benefits of technology solutions first and pay later. While such solutions deliver multiple risk management and operations control benefits, they also pose significant transition challenges.

Integrated SaaS and Outsourced Service

Improved operations control, risk avoidance, and added revenue are the most significant benefits of integrated outsourced and SaaS solutions during both implementation and exploitation phases:

- SaaS requires no large up-front investment in hardware, software licenses, or systems integration on the part of the user.
- SaaS shifts the onus of systems management from the user to the SaaS vendor.

In business accounting terms, SaaS turns capital expense into operating expense, which translates into the following:

- A better balance sheet
- Lower risk, especially during the period of rapid technology innovation on one hand and practice-building stages on the other hand

Transition – People and Processes

Once you've selected your outsourced solution vendor(s) for EMR and billing, you face a transition challenge. It involves people, processes, and technology. Since the SaaS model eliminates traditional systems management headaches, you can focus on only people and processes:

1. **Communicate, communicate, communicate** – The likelihood for implementation success is directly proportional to staff involvement. Review current workflow, understand expected changes, and make sure everybody in the practice agrees with them, including the practice manager, doctors, and office personnel. To avoid errors and conflicts in the future, leave nobody behind using the old workflow. Document the following:

   a. **Steps** required to schedule an appointment: register a patient's arrival; find out an outstanding balance; bring the patient to the exam room; find previous diagnostics, treatment, and financial plans; and gather vital signs, medication, and allergy lists.

   b. **Tasks** required to get paid in full and on time. Include coding, claim submission, denial review, appeals, follow-up with payers and patients, secondary submissions, and a review of accounts receivable.

   c. **Individuals** performing those tasks, locations, and task durations.

2. **Manage expectations** – Laurence J. Peter observed in *The Peter Principle*, "If you don't know where you are going, you will probably end up somewhere else." Document specific changes in the new workflow. Identify specific steps in the new workflow that require fewer or less-qualified resources. Quantify expected benefits in terms of saved resources, added revenue, and personnel savings. Schedule specific timelines for meeting specific financial benchmarks.

3. **Control the fear of change** – Do not force the new system on the old workflow. If the old processes had met practice business requirements, you wouldn't have looked for better solutions. Carefully design the new workflow, leveraging the new solutions together with workflow participants, including the practice manager and every doctor.

4. **Prioritize** – Don't try to implement an entirely new process that includes all new features at once. Soften the transition shock by using a gradual approach, minimizing the amount of changes, but maintaining a steady and sufficiently frequent pace of small changes to complete the transition on time. Avoid scheduling migration to a new system coincidental with the practice move to a new physical location.

5. **Lead** – Without a manager for the entire transition process, members of the transition team will find other priorities and won't take responsibility for delivery. While a technical background or prior familiarity with EMR are helpful, the following leadership skills and a commitment to accomplish results are critical for successful implementation:
   a. Communication
   b. Expectations management
   c. Consensus building and conflict resolution
   d. Delegation
   e. Attention to detail
   f. Verification of delivery

6 **Track** – Schedule regular (weekly) implementation

review meetings with the practice manager to do one of the following:

    a. Ascertain that progress is made according to the plan

    b. Modify the plan

7. **Schedule** – Without specific action items, including specific owners and delivery dates, implementation will drag on and exceed allocated costs. Consider using a process tracking system (e.g., TrackLogix). Pay special attention to the following:

    a. **Payer enrollments** – Fill out required paperwork. Check for clerical errors.

    b. **SOAP note customization** – Review current notes. Consult every doctor in the practice when designing the new templates.

    c. **Custom reporting** – Address any unique practice needs.

    d. **Legacy systems and data** – Review interfaces. Contact vendors. Prioritize record upload.

    e. **Testing** – Design a test plan for specific transition and integration items. Schedule dates.

    f. **Going live** – Find low-volume days to reduce damage from unexpected errors.

    g. **Personnel training** – Focus on the new process. Test newly acquired system skills.

8. **Train gradually** – Allocate enough time to train everybody on both the new processes and the technology. Do not try to jam everything your system can do into a single training session. Expect multiple training ses-

sions, adjusting to the participants' learning pace. Ease in, and use the "onion peel" approach, training personnel on only those features required for the new processes and specific scheduled items on hand:

a. **Basic scheduler and superbill** – Learn to schedule patient appointments, enter demographics for a new patient, test patient eligibility and balance online, and enter charges for a patient visit.

b. **Workbench and problem tracking** – Identify denied claims. Respond to billing operations requests for information, review denied claims, and update claim data.

c. **EMR** – Update SOAP notes. Test drug interaction. Review referral reports.

d. **Basic accountability reports** – Track charges, payments, and billing quality (percent of A/R beyond 120 days). Generate a summary of accounts receivable by payer or a breakdown of revenue by physician for a given month or cumulative to date. Review end-of-day reports for patient visits, new patients, patient visit averages, missed appointments, and accounts receivable.

e. **Advanced EMR** – Modify SOAP note templates. Modify alert generation rules.

f. **Patient relationship management** – Create and track payment plans. Manage patient compliance.

g. **Advanced reporting and performance analysis** – Track payment variations by CPT codes and payers. Identify the worst payer for the best revenue-producing CPT code. Analyze your audit risk exposure. Identify undercoded or overcoded claims.

Chapter 18

Physician Interface to EMR

B illing and claims management services and systems help healthcare providers manage rising costs of healthcare as well as increase overall administrative efficiency. The wider the scope of solution, the more benefit it delivers to the practice. The most important scope enhancement in recent years is the addition of integrated electronic medical records (EMR) solutions, which is the heart of the medical practice-IT value chain. The comprehensive nature of EMR consolidates a patient's personal and administrative information, health history, prescriptions, treatments, and conditions. The ability of EMR to perform such data aggregation at the point of care elevates its benefit from merely recording a patient encounter to creating a useful decision support system.

The most critical part of any system is its interfaces to other systems and, especially, its human interface. Typically, EMR allows three kinds of input: typing, dictation, and point-and-click templates. Most physicians choose dictation over typing and point-and-click templates for reasons of convenience and time efficiencies.

While the preference of dictation over typing is obvious, recent technology progress and regulatory compliance pressures make point-and-click templates superior to dictation.

Dictation and Transcription

Medical transcription saves time in comparison to handwritten notes or typing. It intuitively matches the physician's working style and power of personal expression, and it's easy to dictate using a phone, PDA, or dictation machine. Human transcribers or voice recognition systems transcribe the dictation into medical notes.

But transcription has multiple disadvantages:

- **Incompleteness** – If notes are not captured immediately at the point of care, it is too easy to exclude important details.
- **Costly processing** – Report generation using unstructured data is much more time-consuming and expensive.
- **Time delays for accessibility** – It typically takes 12 to 24 hours for chart turnaround.

Note incompleteness is the most important disadvantage of dictation and transcription, because comprehensive medical notes are key to surviving a post-payment insurance audit.

Point-and-Click Templates

A point-and-click template presents a selection of data elements, a navigation mechanism, and a point-and-click process for capturing patient information. The doctor simply points and clicks, selecting appropriate choices while the system fills out a complete record of selections, which makes up the resulting encounter notes. Such a structured approach offers multiple benefits:

1. **Consistency** – Structured data ensures note completeness and avoids missing important details. It enhances the ability to generate clinically useful reports, such as appointment reminders or disease management.
2. **Customization** – The doctor specifies the template layout to precisely match the workflow of the practice.
3. **Lower error rate** – Standardization of input precludes errors of omission or spelling.
4. **Faster decision making** – Similar observations have similar notes, resulting in consistent decisions.
5. **Immediate accessibility for processing** – Since notes are created within the EMR system, they are available immediately upon completion.

However, point-and-click data entry also has several disadvantages:

1. **Complexity** – It takes more effort to create the notes using point-and-click templates than just writing or dictating.
2. **Data entry time** – It may take too long to walk through all the required templates in front of the patient.
3. **Cost** – As each practice has different workflows, template customization may be costly.

The added complexity of point-and-click templates is clearly justifiable because of guaranteed completeness, which is key to regulatory compliance and the ability to survive post-payment audits. The data entry time can also be reduced by allocating a lion's share of the doctor's time to comprehensive documentation during the initial examination and by restricting the documentation scope to note updates only during subsequent visits. The structured nature of point-and-click templates is naturally conducive to such time prioritization.

Summary

Although some physicians prefer familiar over convenient, and convenient over better functionality, transcription must be viewed as an inferior component of the interface array to the modern EMR system, at most playing a complementary role to point-and-click templates. Modern physician office automation technologies combine both billing and EMR features, and they provide both kinds of interfaces, adding to both the efficacy and efficiency of practice workflow. Powerful Vericle-like technologies also facilitate rapid customization of point-and-click templates, optimizing the physician's interface to the EMR system, providing an added degree of regulatory compliance, and reducing post-payment audit risks.

Chapter 19

Result-Driven Patient Care Plan

"Integrated patient relationship management and billing technologies have uniquely addressed horrendous complexities of financial care plan management and become indispensable in building large volume practices," says Dr. Brian Capra, a practicing doctor of chiropractic and director at Advanced Chiropractic in New Jersey.

Financial care plans help the patient to afford the care while establishing a guaranteed cash flow to the provider. The concept of a financial care plan is based on a relative cost difference for the same service during the plan period and outside of it. The patient is guaranteed a lower fee for each service encounter by committing to higher number of service encounters.

A financial care plan plays an important role in patient relationship management because it improves the perception of the cost-benefit of services; without the plan, the cost for the same service would be higher. Therefore, it's important to track the plan for each patient and, upon reaching the end of the plan, immediately charge the regular (higher) fee.

But tracking multiple patient care plans becomes difficult

upon reaching large numbers of patient visits, impeding the continued development of the clinic. Worse, the complexity of individual plan management is exacerbated by varying sources of the payments required for different kinds of visits. For instance, the fee for care during a specific period of time is paid by either the insurance company or the patient. Finally, the number of visits in each plan is variable too, depending on the patient's health condition and specific plan. For example, the number of visits during the care plan period is indefinite, but the number of recommended adjustments is typically finite.

Therefore, chiropractic office billing technology must be able to handle both kinds of complexities. First, it must be able to handle multiple care plans. Second, it must be able to separately allocate different charges to the care plan while managing the combined payment status for the same visit.

Care Plan Definition

A powerful care plan management system maintains three kinds of edits: addition of a service encounter without adding a charge, addition of a plan payment without adding a service encounter, and addition of both a service and a payment. Also, if the current plan is paid in full at the beginning of the plan, the service charges during the care period must be discounted.

A care plan is defined by three components: time period, total amount of charges and payments, and total number of services provided to the patient. Services include adjustments, but they often exclude X-rays and exams—and they always exclude supplies, such as pillows or vitamins. To define a care plan in a Vericle-like system, do the following:

1. Select the patient

2. Select the care plan start and end dates
3. Update the maximum plan visits
4. Update the maximum care plan amount
5. Update expected insurance payments
6. Update the deductible
7. Select one of the following billing options:
   a. Bill patient only (no insurance charge)
   b. Bill insurance upon exceeding patient's maximum care plan amount
   c. Bill patient upon exceeding maximum care plan amount, and write off patient's portion

Care Plan Status

Chiropractic office management systems must be able to show the status of the care plan, which includes the following:

- Visits
- Charges
- Payments
- Write-offs
- Balance

Note that the care plan status must be available to both the provider and the front desk person, who will be able to discuss any outstanding balance with the patient upon arrival at the office. A colored display of relevant information helps the front desk person to react quickly and effectively to situations that require correction—e.g., bad plan definition dates, missing visit data, or an unpaid balance.

Care Plan Tracking

To begin charging a patient regular fees or to define a new care plan upon care plan expiration, the office must track the care plan end dates. Such a care plan expiration tracking function is accomplished in two ways:

- Today's appointment list shows patients with expired care plans.
- A separate report lists patients with expired care plans within a given date range.

Summary

In summary, a financial care plan is an important component of a practice-building strategy as it helps the patient to afford the care while establishing a guaranteed cash flow to the provider. But tracking multiple patient care plans becomes difficult upon reaching large numbers of patient visits, impeding the continued development of the clinic. Outsourced billing services that leverage integrated technology help the chiropractic clinic overcome care plan management complexity and build a successful large-volume practice.

Part IV

Compliance and Audit

It was much pleasanter at home, when one wasn't always growing larger and smaller, and being ordered about by mice and rabbits.

—Alice
Alice's Adventures in Wonderland
Lewis Carroll

Compliance and audit risk services improve with each additional practice using Vericle. Vericle leverages the network effect to improve these services in several ways, which are discussed in this part. It presents two chapters, one focused on HIPAA compliance and the other on medical note management compliance. Both issues are crucially important for practice management, and both must be handled effectively and unobtrusively, without impeding practice productivity.

HIPAA compliance emphasizes security and privacy, while medical note management compliance emphasizes medical necessity. Accordingly, HIPAA compliance employs mostly technical tools and procedures to lock information away and to ensure secure access on a "need to know" basis, while medical note compliance procedures use technology and processes to track medical progress and monitor potential payment rule violation likelihood and audit exposure. At the end, the successful implementation of both HIPAA and medical note compliance depends on discipline and adequate technology.

Chapter 20

HIPAA Compliance and Role-Based Access Control

H IPAA compliance requires special focus and effort, as failure to comply carries significant risk of damage and penalties. A practice with multiple separate systems for patient scheduling, electronic medical records, and billing requires multiple separate HIPAA management efforts. This chapter presents an integrated approach to HIPAA compliance and outlines key HIPAA terminology, principles, and requirements to help the practice owner ensure HIPAA compliance by medical billing services and software vendors.

The last decade of the previous century witnessed accelerating proliferation of digital technology in healthcare, which, along with reduced costs and greater service quality, introduced new and greater risks for accidental disclosure of personal health information.

The Health Insurance Portability and Accountability Act (HIPAA) was passed in 1996 by Congress to establish national standards for privacy and security of personal health data. The

Privacy Rule, a component of HIPAA written by the U.S. Department of Health and Human Services, took effect on April 14, 2003.

Failure to comply with HIPAA risks accreditation and reputation damage, lawsuits by the federal government, financial penalties (ranging from $100 to $250,000), and imprisonment (ranging from one year to ten years).

Protected Health Information (PHI)

The key term of HIPAA is protected health information (PHI), which includes anything that can be used to identify an individual and any information shared with other healthcare providers or clearinghouses in any media (digital, verbal, recorded voice, faxed, printed, or written). Information that can be used to identify an individual includes the following:

1. Name
2. Dates (except year)
3. ZIP code of more than 3 digits, telephone and fax numbers, email address
4. Social Security numbers
5. Medical record numbers
6. Health plan numbers
7. License numbers
8. Photographs

Information shared with other healthcare providers or clearinghouses include the following:

1. Nursing and physician notes
2. Billing and other treatment records

PRACTICING PROFITABILITY

Principles of HIPAA

HIPAA intends to allow the smooth flow of PHI for healthcare operations subject to a patient's consent, but it prohibits any flow of unauthorized PHI for any other purposes. Healthcare operations include treatment, payment, care quality assessment, competence review training, accreditation, insurance rating, auditing, and legal procedures.

HIPAA promotes fair information practices and requires those with access to PHI to safeguard it. Fair information practices means that a patient must be allowed the following:

1. Access to PHI
2. Correction for errors and completeness
3. Knowledge of others who use PHI

Safeguarding of PHI means that anybody who holds PHI must meet these requirements:

1. Be accountable for its use and disclosure
2. Have a legal recourse to combat violations

HIPAA Implementation Process

HIPAA implementation begins upon making assumptions about the PHI disclosure threat model. The implementation includes both preemptive and retroactive controls, and it involves process, technology, and personnel aspects.

A threat model helps an understanding of the purpose of the HIPAA implementation process. It includes assumptions about the following:

1. Threat nature (e.g., accidental disclosure by insiders, access for profit)
2. Source of threat (e.g., outsider or insider)
3. Means of potential threat (e.g., break-in, physical intrusion, computer hack, virus)
4. Specific kind of data at risk (e.g., patient identification, financials, or medical records)
5. Scale (e.g., how many patient records are threatened)

The HIPAA process must include a clearly stated policy, educational materials and events, a clear enforcement means, a schedule for testing of HIPAA compliance, and a means for the continued transparency about HIPAA compliance. A stated policy typically includes a statement of least privilege (the least amount of privileged data necessary to complete the job), the definition of PHI, and incident monitoring and reporting procedures. Educational materials may include case studies, control questions, and a schedule of review seminars for personnel.

Technology Requirements for HIPAA Compliance

Technology implementation of HIPAA proceeds in stages, from logical data definition to the physical data center to the network.

1. **To assure physical data center security**, the manager must do the following:
   a. Lock the data center
   b. Manage the access list
   c. Track data center access with closed-circuit TV cameras to monitor both internal and external building activities

    d. Protect access to the data center with 24/7 on-site security

    e. Protect backup data

    f. Test the recovery procedure

2. **For network security**, the data center must have special facilities for the following:

    a. Secure networking – firewall protection, encrypted data transfer only

    b. Network access monitoring and report auditing

3. **For data security**, the manager must have the following:

    a. Individual authentication – individual logins and passwords

    b. Role-based access control (see below)

    c. Audit trails – all access to all data fields tracked and recorded

    d. Data discipline – limited ability to download data

Role-Based Access Control (RBAC)

RBAC improves the convenience and flexibility of systems management. Greater convenience helps reduce the errors of commission and omission in granting access privileges to users. Greater flexibility helps implement the policy of least privilege, where the users are granted only as many privileges as are required in order to complete their jobs.

RBAC promotes economies of scale, because the frequency of changes of role definition for a single user is higher than the frequency of changes of role definitions across an entire organization. Thus, to make a massive change of privileges for a large number of users with the same set of privileges, the administrator only makes changes to the role definition.

Hierarchical RBAC also promotes economies of scale and reduces the likelihood of errors. It allows redefining roles by inheriting privileges assigned to roles in the higher hierarchical level.

RBAC is based on establishing a set of user profiles or roles according to responsibilities. Each role has a predefined set of privileges. The user acquires privileges by receiving membership in the role or assignment of a profile by the administrator.

Every time the definition of the role changes along with the set of privileges that is required to complete the job associated with the role, the administrator needs only to redefine the privileges of the role. The privileges of all of the users who have this role are automatically redefined.

Similarly, if the role of a single user is changed, the only operation that needs to be performed is the reassignment of the user profile, which will automatically redefine the user's access privileges according to the new profile.

Summary

HIPAA compliance requires special practice management attention. A practice with multiple and separate systems for scheduling, electronic medical records, and billing requires multiple and separate HIPAA management efforts. An integrated system reduces the complexity of HIPAA implementation. By outsourcing technology to a HIPAA-compliant vendor of a Vericle-like technology solution on an ASP or SaaS basis, HIPAA management overhead can be eliminated.

Chapter 21

Pre-Payment and Post-Payment Audits

Mistaken payments add up to an estimated $200 billion, exceeding 10% of national healthcare costs. Other party liability (OPL) alone—i.e., claims that should be paid by somebody else—comprise $68 billion, or 3.6% of national healthcare costs. The enormity of potential savings due to improved claims processing continues to attract the attention and focus of resources. Insurance profitability experts believe that a payment scrutiny program can be as successful a profit-building strategy for insurance companies as raising premiums or adding members. A growing industry of outsourced technology and services to avoid mistaken payments is also symptomatic of the growing demand for such services. Some vendors cite cumulative payment savings as high as $3 billion.

However, avoiding mistaken payments is difficult because of four-pronged constraints: the volume of claims, the disparate and disconnected sources of relevant information, the resource-intensive manual processes needed to identify and investigate recovery opportunities, and regulatory requirements for timely payments.

To manage these difficulties, many payers adopted a two-phase-based "pay and refund" approach for payment minimization. The second phase of this approach is designed to correct any mistakes made during the first phase. Each of the phases can be further divided into two subphases. Specifically, the initial phase splits into pre-payment review and timely payment of valid items, while the final phase includes post-payment audits and refunds of items proven invalid during the audit.

Pre-Payment Review

Pre-payment review typically proceeds in two stages: identification and confirmation. Potential overpayment identification requires cross-referencing multiple systems that manage provider enrollment, authorizations, recovery case management, and call centers for both insured and providers.

Overpayment confirmation uses Correct Coding Initiative (CCI), local medical review policies (LMRPs), and other rules to categorize the potential overpayments into contractual/clinical, eligibility, coordination of benefits, or duplicate payments. Overpayment confirmation typically includes tests for inter-claim, intra-claim, or cross-claim inconsistencies; lifetime duplicates; date range duplicates; re-bundling; inappropriate modifier codes; wrong E&M crosswalk; upcoded or undercoded visit level; etc.

Pre-payment review requires powerful database technology. Most of the pre-payment claim review process can be automated along with the subsequent denial notice or explanation of benefits (EOB).

Post-Payment Audit

In contrast, post-payment audits tend to consume more re-sources during each one of the audit stages:

1. **Target identification** – An audit identification re-port shows total annual revenue and the degree of variance between the audit target and peers in the same specialty and geography. The product of the two numbers is proportional to the expected gain from the audit, essentially providing a natural audit ranking (Figure 8).

Figure 8. Statistical Audit Flagging

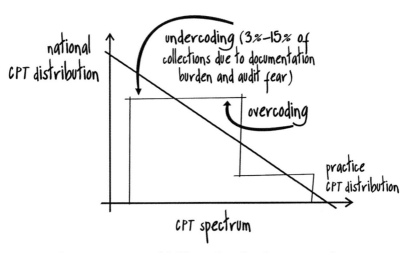

Superposition of billing distributions reveals patterns of nonconformity.

2. **Audit preparation** – A higher return to the payer is the key advantage of a carefully designed and executed post-payment audit. Audit preparation starts with a

review of the audit target selection, which is the result of provider profiling and variance reporting. This stage includes a list of claims paid in the past that are most likely to fall outside of a standard distribution of the peer group.

3. **Audit execution** – The auditor requests and analyzes medical notes supporting the data reflected in the sample of paid claims that are produced at the audit preparation stage. The auditor's objective is to establish the proportion of claims found unsupported by reviewed medical notes within the set of the audited sample (percent of overpayment).

4. **Refund (and penalty) extrapolation** – The auditor extrapolates the refund as the product of the percent of overpayment and the total payments by the auditing insurance carrier for the past six years.

5. **Negotiation**

6. **Settlement**

Some stages—such as audit execution, negotiation, and settlement—must be entirely manual and may require highly skilled and experienced personnel. Other stages—such as verification of overpayment amount and currency, identification of overpayment reason, and audit prioritization—may be partially automated, using rule-based technology to identify procedure repetition, high payments per day, surge analysis, unusual modifiers, unusual procedure rates, geographic improbabilities, or 5/50 patterns. External resources might be added at this stage to consult provider watch lists, OIG sanctions databases, or high-risk address databases.

Summary

A full-scale implementation of payment scrutiny requires sophisticated processes to handle pre-payment claim reviews and post-payment audits, and such processes use advanced fraud detection technology. Pre-payment claim reviews are less expensive than post-payment audits and therefore can be applied to every claim, while post-payment audits must be carefully targeted. A system to manage the overpayment recovery process must include claim identification, claim history, provider and insured information, medical notes, insured services call center notes, authorizations, etc. Without the ability to efficiently manage a large volume of recovery cases, the risk for errors or missed payment deadlines is high, resulting in missed recovery opportunities.

Part V

Metrics, Analysis, and Reporting

It would be so nice if something made sense for a change.

—Alice
Alice's Adventures in Wonderland
Lewis Carroll

Vericle achieves the network effect by combining STP (Straight-Through Processing) methodology with the SaaS (Software as a Service) software delivery method. STP methodology is rooted in the comprehensive measurement of every aspect of the billing process and in continuous process improvement discipline.

This part starts with a critical review of various medical billing performance metrics in Chapter 22. Chapter 23 introduces the concept of billing transparency and Vericle's dashboard. Patient relationship management and financial care plan reporting are presented in Chapter 24. End-of-day reports as well as missed and unbilled appointment reduction techniques are discussed in Chapter 25. Chapter 26 discusses the process and associated reports for structured denial management. The final chapter presents OLAP concepts and second-order SQL queries for lost revenue recovery under the advanced topics framework.

Chapter 22

Service Performance Metrics

B illing performance measurement is an integral part of the medical practice billing process and a prerequisite to effective practice management. Systematic measurement becomes mission-critical with the growth of billing complexity or outsourcing of the billing function. Traditional billing metrics are limited in scope; they focus on the claim submission process, ignoring process imperfections on the insurance (payer) side. Modern computer technologies allow both productive measurement and effective action by the disciplined billing office to improve claim submission and payment processes.

Using appropriate metrics helps improve policies and procedures, shorten revenue cycles, reduce patient complaints, improve financial performance and compliance, increase cash flow, reduce bad debt, identify areas of potential growth, improve employee morale, increase productivity, and reduce costs. Useful metrics must be comprehensive and simple. They must combine both complete end-to-end processes and the individual components of those processes. Metrics must be used consistently over time and compared to standards. Obviously, different standards apply to different medical specialties, patient demographics, payers, and samples of CPT codes.

Medical billing metrics typically include compliance, cash balances, charges, accounts receivable, and collection ratios to help monitor cash flow. This chapter focuses on performance metrics.

Collection Ratios

Traditional metrics include gross and net collection ratios. Both metrics are subjective to the individual practice because they compare (often arbitrary) charges to (allowed) payments. (Net collection rate is defined as the ratio of total collections and total charges less adjustments. Gross collection rate is defined as the ratio of total collections to total charges only.) According to the Medical Group Management Association (MGMA) 1998 Cost Survey, adjusted fee-for-service collections (net collections) for family practices in 1997 averaged 98.65%. A declining net collection ratio may be symptomatic of increased contractual write-offs or an insufficient number of denial appeals. This metric is especially useful in the absence of modern computer technology, when comparison of every payment to the allowed amount is impossible, or when the appeals process of denials is too expensive. Otherwise, the use of charges in defining gross and net collection metrics precludes them from the productive discovery of process improvement opportunities.

Days in Accounts Receivable (DAR)

A growing number of days in accounts receivable is symptomatic of a faulty billing process. One way to determine DAR is to count days from the date of service to the date of payment for every claim and then average that across all claims. A simpler way to compute average number of days in accounts receivable is by taking a ratio of accounts receivable to average daily charges, or

No. of Days in Accounts Receivable =
(Accounts Receivable / Average Charge) x 365

This metric also depends on the medical specialty, patient demographics, payer mix, and CPT sample. Another downside is that this metric is sensitive to the provider because it counts the lag time of unsubmitted claims for services already delivered. This lag time roughly averages across all payers, making DAR an effective comparison metric between payers for an individual provider, but invalidating it across multiple providers.

One obvious advantage of the DAR metric is its independence of charges. The averaging feature of this metric eliminates sensitivity to a specific day or CPT, but it also hides the behavior shape of the accounts receivable curve.

First-Pass Pay (FPP) Rate and Denial Rate

The FPP rate is the percentage of claims paid in full upon the first submission (subject to federal or state timely payment regulations: 15 days for electronic submission and 30 days for paper).

The denial rate is the complementary metric to the FPP rate. It counts the percentage of claims that require follow-up and therefore cost more to process. Follow-up may take the form of a phone call to the payer to discover a lost claim or to receive interpretation of a denial message, correction of earlier submitted data, resubmission of the original claim, consultation with the provider and medical notes, or denial appeal.

Both FPP and denial rates are very important metrics often used for billing process improvement. The upside of the FPP/denial metric is that it is charge-invariant, but its downside is that it hides the differences between process imperfections on the claim submission and claim payment sides. To identify patterns of problem CPT codes or payers, the FPP/denial metric needs to be computed and compared across all payer-CPT code pairs, which is a standard feature for modern billing technologies.

Patient Liability

The percentage of patient liability is the ratio of patient responsibility to total billed charges, and it roughly reflects patient deductibles. This metric is important in measuring front office function because it has little to do with clean claim submission or effective follow-up.

Percentage of Accounts Receivable Beyond X Days (PARBX)

PARBX resolves the sensitivity issue of the DAR metric and offers a simple and charge-invariant metric of the billing process. Its graphic representation has a skewed bell shape (Figures 9 and 10).

Its steepness represents billing process quality; a steep curve and thin tail means a healthy billing process, while a flat bell and fat tail means billing problems. According to the MGMA survey, 25%–35% of the average family practice's accounts receivables were more than 120 days old in 1997. This number has improved down to 17.7% in 2004 (Lowes, 2004).

Figure 9. Bad Billing Performance

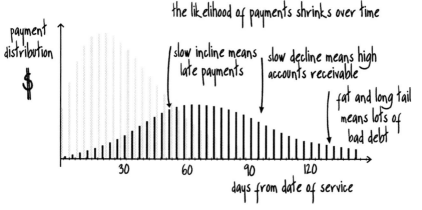

bad billing performance has fat and long tail and slow incline and decline

the likelihood of payments shrinks over time

payment distribution
$

slow incline means late payments

slow decline means high accounts receivable

fat and long tail means lots of bad debt

30   60   90   120

days from date of service

The likelihood of payment shrinks with each passing day.

Figure 10. Good Billing Performance

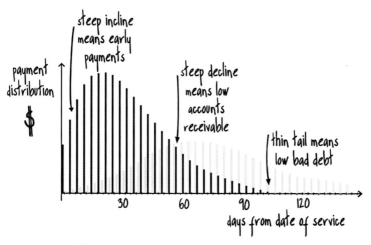

good billing performance has thin tail and steep incline and decline

steep incline means early payments

payment distribution
$

steep decline means low accounts receivable

thin tail means low bad debt

30   60   90   120

days from date of service

The sooner the payments are received,
the more likely it is that every claim will be paid in full.

Summary

In summary, comprehensive and charge-invariant metrics, such as PARBX, are more informative and objective than collection ratios. However, these metrics alone fall short of identifying specific areas for billing process improvement. Modern technology helps to identify billing bottlenecks as it allows the interactive review of multiple metrics along different aggregation dimensions. For instance, the PARBX metric is especially helpful to identify patterns of problem claims containing specific payers or CPT codes. Further, modern Vericle-like technologies enable the comparison of every payment to the allowed amount and subsequent appeal on every denial, effectively reducing the average percentage of accounts receivable to low single digits.

Chapter 23

Billing Transparency

Arcane terminology and complex rules for payer- and time-dependent claim validity and pricing interpretation plague the medical billing industry. This results in massive payments of invalid or ineligible claims and in denials of error-free claims. The amount and complexity of billing information make it very difficult for the doctor to maintain compliance and to identify and resolve errors and underpayments.

"With integrated Billing Transparency, I see for myself how Vericle leverages every opportunity to expedite payments of healthcare insurance claims in a continuous 24/7 effort. It has enabled 27% revenue gain over [the] past billing process," says Doug Cassel, MD, director of Interventional Radiology at Hoag Memorial Hospital in Newport Beach, California.

Greater visibility of internal process activities promotes teamwork, increases client satisfaction, and assists in process streamlining. Billing service transparency allows participants of the billing process to expedite error identification and resolution, resulting in reduced overpayments and underpayments and in improved regulatory compliance.

Billing Dashboard as Main Transparency Mechanism

Selection of meaningful and intuitive indicators for the billing process performance is a mission-critical stage in creating a useful transparency mechanism. A "dashboard" presenting the most meaningful data must be easy to find and simple to interpret. The cumulative experience of hundreds of doctors using Vericle has shown that a dashboard containing nine specific indicators expedites the development of intuitive and powerful transparency mechanisms:

1. Month-to-date collections
2. Total failed or denied claims
3. Aggregate failed or denied claims in the follow-up queue
4. Dollar amount of accounts receivable (A/R) below 30 days
5. Dollar amount of A/R from 31–120 days
6. Dollar amount of A/R greater than 120 days
7. Percentage of A/R below 30 days
8. Percentage of A/R from 31–120 days
9. Percentage of A/R greater than 120 days

Note that the national average of accounts receivable above 120 days hovers around 18% (Lowes, 2004). Therefore, a well-performing outsourced billing service must deliver an A/R above 120 days that's significantly below 18%. Specifically, to justify its fees, an outsourced billing service must measure its A/R above 120 days at somewhere around 5%.

Drill-down Functionality, Reporting, and Transparency

An advanced dashboard allows a drill-down for more detail by pointing and clicking directly on the screen. At the minimum, the following features must be available:

- **Operational report** – Shows total claims and dollar amounts submitted, paid, adjusted, written off, and failed. It allows a breakdown by CPT code, payer, referral, or a combination of such dimensions.
- **Denials report** – Shows the list of denied claims and a log of follow-up actions. When sorting it by the amount paid, you can determine the smallest payment that the billing service will fight for.
- **Compliance report** – Shows the potential for post-payment audit and itemizes compliance violations.

These reports allow multiple dimensions for data presentation by single parameter—such as payer, CPT code, provider, or referring physician—or by more complex parameter combinations—such as pairs of payer-CPT code, provider-CPT code, or referring physician-CPT code.

Complexity Considerations

Note that even a small single-provider practice working with 20 CPT codes and 20 payers will have 400 (20 x 20) payer-CPT code pairs. Therefore, an online report comparing month-to-date collections between current and previous years requires a powerful database query capability. Moreover, automation of such queries—like "find the worst-performing payer for the best-performing CPT code"—requires OLAP (online analytical processing) technology.

Summary

Billing transparency is a necessary feature of a modern and accountable billing service. Billing transparency allows the practice owner to know both the big picture and the minute detail of the billing process. To be able to observe every step of the billing process on a continuous 24/7 basis, reporting must be available using a secure, HIPAA-compliant connection over the Internet. While traditional services have delivered monthly paper reports, modern technology allows the delivery of continuously updated and meaningful billing performance data.

Chapter 24

Patient Relationship Management

The key value proposition of patient relationship management, or PRM (also known as customer relationship management, or CRM, outside of healthcare), is its ability to enhance financial performance of the clinic by helping retain current patients and attract new patients. PRM helps provide timely, patient-centered, and efficient care, emphasizing preventive instead of reactive care. PRM is a data-driven and patient-focused methodology to strategic practice building and effective patient relationship development.

PRM helps identify new service needs, and then helps design care programs and processes for front office and billing functions to meet those needs. A PRM system captures patient information during the entire period of each care plan in terms of functional health improvement, care plan implementation, and billing.

Patient Relationship Management Concept

PRM is based on a simple concept of monitoring and responding to practice workflow data. Effective PRM integrates key data structures, including the patient's travel card (SOAP notes), financial care plan, and billing (charges, payments, and balance).

A PRM system tracks changes in the key data structures and generates "alert" reports to office management about patients reaching critical thresholds. The office manager and the doctor review such reports and respond according to the practice's development strategy, using call centers, the Internet, direct mail, or personal conversations during office visits.

Financial Care Plan

A financial care plan is an effective tool for patient loyalty development because it helps the patient to afford the care while establishing a guaranteed cash flow to the provider. Patient loyalty is enhanced because of a financial incentive offered to the patient.

The concept of a financial care plan is based on the relative cost difference for the same service during the plan period and outside of that period. The patient is guaranteed a certain number of free service encounters by committing to a care plan.

A financial care plan improves the perception of service costs and benefits, because without the plan, the cost for the same number of service encounters would be higher. Therefore, it is important to track the plan for each patient and, upon reaching the end of the plan, begin charging the regular fee.

1. **End-of-Day Report** – An end-of-day report displays new patients, visits, cash, insurance, free services, insurance (billed, collected), cash collected, missed appointments, recalls, and patient visit average. An end-of-day report is the main report of PRM because it allows the manager to reconcile revenues with patient

visits, eliminating no-charge visits and unbillable appointments. An end-of-day report also provides an interactive "drill in" ability to reach an electronic travel card and financial care plan.

2. **Electronic Travel Card** – An electronic equivalent of a paper travel card, the electronic travel card (ETC) contains complete information about a patient's health and care history. It's similar to the electronic medical record and subject to the same HIPAA compliance regulations. An ETC includes the following:
   a. Numbers and dates of visits
   b. SOAP notes for each visit
   c. ICD-9 and CPT codes
   d. Care frequency recommendation summary
   e. X-rays and posture images

3. **Financial Care Plan Status Report** – A chiropractic office management system must be able to show the status of the financial care plan, including the following:
   a. Visits
   b. Charges
   c. Payments
   d. Write-offs
   e. Balance

Note that both the provider and the front desk person use the care plan status report, since the front desk person must be able to discuss any outstanding balance with the patient upon arrival at the office. A colored display of relevant information helps the front desk person react quickly and effectively to situations that require correction—e.g., bad plan definition dates, missing visit data, or an unpaid balance.

4. **Care Plan Tracking** – To begin charging patients regular fees or to define a new care plan upon care plan expiration, the office must track care plan end dates. Such a care plan expiration tracking function is accomplished in two ways:
   a. Today's appointment list shows patients with expired care plans.
   b. A separate report lists patients with expired care plans within a given date range.

Summary

Patient relationship management is a catalyst for building successful and competitive chiropractic clinics. Integrated systems that combine data about a patient's health, care plans, and billing are the cornerstone for patient relationship management. A disciplined practice manager reviews end-of-day and financial care tracking reports daily to monitor and reconcile average patient visits, missed appointments, recalls, new patients, charges, and collections.

Chapter 25

No-Show Risk Management

Most clinics lose an average of 20% of their revenue due to missed appointments. Lost revenue may not be the largest problem clinics face due to no-shows. Other problems span health damage, patient liability risks, reduced accessibility, and impeded resident education. Rigorous no-show management methods utilizing powerful Vericle-like technologies, which integrate scheduling and billing data, reduce no-show rates and improve associated revenues by more than 50% (Hashim et al., 2001).

No-Show Frequency Distribution

No-show rates average about 20%: 10% of clinics have less than 10% no-shows, 42% of clinics have 10%–20%, 34% of clinics have 20%–30%, and 14% of clinics have more than 30% no-shows. Further, the top 10 clinics in terms of lowest no-show rates range from 3%–9% for no-shows, while the bottom 10 clinics reach 33%–57% (Moore, 2001).

No-Show Impact to Clinic

A missed appointment poses five kinds of problems:

1. **Health damage** – A patient's health can be damaged due to interrupted continuity of care or a missed opportunity to solve an acute health problem. The doctor also loses an opportunity for a timely review of patient health, treatment progress, etc.

2. **Liability risk** – A patient who misses an appointment and suffers an injury may have a viable cause for a lawsuit against the practice. To avoid such risk, the doctor must maintain evidence of giving clear directions and making reasonable efforts to ensure the patient's compliance with the care program, including keeping follow-up appointments.

3. **Reduced accessibility** – Other patients are postponed and do not get access to care because of a no-show or canceled appointment.

4. **Impedance to resident education** – A resident doctor misses an opportunity to hone care skills.

5. **Loss of revenue** – The clinic is unable to make up revenue due to missed appointments.

Three-Phase No-Show Management Strategy

An effective no-show management strategy is based on tracking, rescheduling, and follow-up:

1. **Tracking**
   a. Record all no-shows, and reconcile them with billing on a daily basis
   b. Record no-show reasons and follow-up notes in patient records
   c. Review end-of-day reports daily

2. **Rescheduling in real time**
   a. Allow patients to request appointments online using the Internet
   b. Overbook, and use waiting lists
   c. Fill new openings with walk-ins or patients from the waiting list

3. **Follow-up**
   a. Activate a sequence of reminder calls/emails to all patients 10 days, 2 days, and 1 day prior to their appointments
   b. Place a follow-up call to determine reasons for no-shows, and reschedule the patient
   c. Follow up with warning letters after one no-show
   d. Dismiss patients from the practice after three no-shows

Reminder calls or emails prior to an appointment remain the most effective method to prevent missed appointments. Additionally, sending reminders via email and allowing patients to confirm online turns an office reminder into a patient's action item, significantly outperforming the impact of a voice message or postcard.

Note that outsourcing reminder calls to calling services and using the Internet reduce the cost of reminders. Therefore reaching **all** patients prior to their appointments makes good business sense.

Three technologies are especially useful in implementing the no-show management strategy outlined above:

1. **End-of-day report** – End-of-day reports display new patients, visits, cash, insurance, free visits, insurance (billed, collected), cash collected, missed appointments, recalls, patient visit average. An end-of-day report allows the manager to reconcile revenues with patient visits, eliminating no-charge visits and unbillable appointments.

2. **Scheduler**
   a. Allows patients access to an Internet-based appointment scheduler
   b. Updates the available appointment list due to cancellations
   c. Alerts about new openings for patients on the waiting list
   d. Alerts about appointments with missing authorizations
   e. Most schedulers allow monthly, weekly, and daily views. The "today" view should change colors for no-show appointments, prompting the front office person to follow up immediately or at the end of the day

3. **Search feature** – A search feature must allow you to find all no-shows within a specific time interval subject to specific patient names, attending physicians,

CPT and/or ICD-9 code combinations, or other demographic conditions. Upon finding specific appointments, a "drill down" should be available to see the related appointment history or recurring appointment plan.

Chapter 26

Claim Denial Management

Partial denials cause the average medical practice to lose as much as 11% of its revenue. Denial management is difficult because of the complexity of denial causes, payer variety, and claim volume. Systematic denial management requires measurement, early claim validation, comprehensive monitoring, and custom appeal process tracking.

In a high-volume clinic, the only practical way to manage denials is to use computer technology and follow a four-step procedure:

1. **Prevent mistakes during claim submission** – This can be accomplished with a built-in claim validation procedure that includes payer-specific tests. Such tests ("pre-submission scrubbing") compare every claim with Correct Coding Initiative (CCI) regulations; diligently review modifiers used to differentiate between procedures on the same claim; and compare the charged amount with the allowed amount, according to previous experience or the previous contract, to

avoid undercharging.

2. **Identify underpayments** – Underpayment identification involves comparing the payment with the allowed amount, identifying zero-paid items, and evaluating payment timeliness. The results of this stage should be displayed in a comprehensive underpayment report sorted by payer, provider, claim identification, and the amount of underpayment.

3. **Appeal denials** – Appeal management includes appeal prioritization, preparation of arguments and documentation, tracking, and escalation. Note that CCI spells out bundling standards, but the number of standard interpretations grows in step with the number of payers. Therefore, CCI provides the justification basis for an appeal, and every appeal must be argued on its own merits, including medical notes. The denial appeal process is typically managed with a custom process tracking system, such as TrackLogix.

4. **Measure denial rates** – You cannot manage what you do not measure. By measuring denial rates and observing payment trends, you can see if your process requires modifications.

Denial risk is not uniform across all claims. Certain classes of claims run significantly higher denial risks, depending on the claim complexity, temporary constraints, and payer idiosyncrasies:

1. **Claim complexity**
   a. Modifiers
   b. Multiple line items

2. **Temporary constraints**
   a. Patient constraint (e.g., claim submission during global periods)
   b. Payer constraint (e.g., claim submission timing proximity to start of fiscal year)
   c. Procedure constraint (e.g., experimental services)

3. **Payer idiosyncrasies**
   a. Bundled services
   b. Disputed medical necessity

First, for complex claims, most payers pay the full amount for one line item, but only a percentage of the remaining items. This payment approach creates two opportunities for underpayment:

1. The order of paid items
2. The payment percentage of remaining items

Next, temporary constraints often cause payment errors because of the misapplication of constraints. For instance, claims submitted during the global period for services unrelated to the global period are often denied. Similar mistakes may occur at the start of the fiscal year because of the misapplication of rules for deductibles or outdated fee schedules.

Finally, payers often vary in their interpretations of Correct Coding Initiative (CCI) bundling rules or coverage of certain services. Developing sensitivity to such idiosyncrasies is a key to full and timely payments.

Summary

Powerful Vericle-like technology helps you manage denial appeals nationwide and stay current until problem resolution is complete. Every time one billing problem is solved, the newly gained knowledge is encoded for recycling. Sharing billing expertise in a central billing knowledge base expedites future problem resolution.

Chapter 27

Lost Revenue Discovery with OLAP

The average medical practice may lose as much as 11% of its revenue due to underpayments. But underpayment recovery potential averages only 5% of revenue and involves a costly appeal process. To avoid unrecoverable losses, some providers discontinue servicing patients insured by the worst-performing payers. Unfortunately, such a drastic loss-reduction measure may boomerang and increase losses, depending on the complexity of referral relationships. This chapter outlines limitations of traditional database queries that are used to identify payer candidates for contract termination and demonstrates alternative decision choices with superior performance, in terms of revenue and risk management, facilitated with online analytical processing (OLAP) technology.

First-Order SQL Queries for A/R Analysis

Traditional accounts receivable analysis includes identifying payers that systematically underpay and refuse denial appeals. Such analysis is based on simple queries that are designed to identify the best CPT code or the worst payer in absolute terms:

- Comparison of revenue for various CPT codes for a given time period
- Comparison of underpayments for various payers for a given time period
- Comparison of denials for various payers for a given time period

Single-key database indexing is a standard measure to improve the time performance of such queries. It builds an ordered relationship within the data elements, based on the value of the selected metric. But single-key indexing precludes the implementation of more complex queries, like "Who is the payer that underpays the most for the best CPT code?" or "Who is the worst referring physician for my worst payer?" And single-key indexing requires complex SQL programming skills because of the need to store and process intermediate results. Therefore, ranking the data elements along a single attribute forces a limited choice for management decision:

- Ignore the problem
- Renegotiate the contract with the payer
- Stop serving patients insured by the worst payer

But to find more subtle solutions, the office manager requires the ability to aggregate and drill into data and formulate queries in real time, in response to observed results to the previous queries. Specifically, a low-frequency, underperforming payer with a high degree of underpayment may not be as detrimental to the office as a high-frequency, underperforming payer with a low degree of underpayment. Contract termination with a wrong payer may accomplish the opposite result for practice goals in terms of revenue maximization and workload reduction. Additionally, a decision to stop serving patients insured by any one payer may cause a reduction of referral volume of other patients across all payers for a particular referring physician.

Combinatorial (Second-Order SQL) Queries

Fortunately, modern database query technology can address both limitations by enabling "second-order SQL" queries, which allow data manipulation based on multiple criteria and using combinations of such criteria.

In our case, second-degree SQL queries allow finding the worst payer for the best revenue-generating code. Such a discriminating approach allows focusing on higher-priority items first, resulting in more effective management. In general, the manager performs a custom comparison of payers according to the following four-step sequence:

1. Select metrics (e.g., percent paid, percent accounts receivable beyond 120 days, percent denials)
2. Select dimensions (providers, payers, CPT codes, ICD-9 codes, referring physicians)
3. Partition
4. Aggregate, drill down, pivot

Worst Payer Query

To find a payer with the highest amount of underpayments for the most-frequent CPT code, a second-order SQL query can be written along the following lines:

For a given time-interval,
Select payers
Where the sum of underpayments over
(all CPT codes where Revenue > Revenue Threshold)
> Underpayment Threshold

Worst Referring Physician Query

To avoid the risk of losing referrals from better-performing payers, the manager may consider severing the referral relationship with some referring physicians instead of payers. In such a case, the distribution of patients across various payers plays an important role for each referring physician. A single combinatorial query may fetch the worst referring physician as follows:

For a given time-interval,
Select referring physicians
Where Revenue for the Worst Payer > Threshold

Summary

Underpayment management involves all phases of claims processing and requires powerful Vericle-like computing platforms for exhaustive comparisons of payments versus allowed amounts and subsequent appeal management. OLAP (online analytical processing) allows better analysis of accounts receivable and more effective management because of the ability to handle queries with functions of multiple attributes and dimensions. Note that in the absence of a native OLAP mechanism, effective Vericle-like billing platforms allow similarly powerful analysis by introducing intermediary steps. Such steps may add insight to analysis and improve decision quality.

Part VI

Outsourcing

If everybody minded their own business, the world would go around a great deal faster than it does.

—The Duchess
Alice's Adventures in Wonderland
Lewis Carroll

Outsourcing is one of the most promising growth directions for billing, given the opportunities for cross-continental labor arbitrage, limited resources within each individual medical practice, and centralized, Internet-based Vericle billing technology. This part starts with a presentation of a "total cost solution" approach. Chapter 29 analyzes the most frequent myths and facts about outsourced billing, including the introduction of a zero-game sum argument. Chapter 30 discusses SaaS (Software as a Service) concepts in the context of patient relationship management. Outsourced lockbox selection is presented in Chapter 31. The final chapter presents a formal problem-tracking process and the underlying technology between a medical practice and an outsourced billing service provider.

Chapter 28

Relative Value
Price-Performance Calculation

Internet-based technology has been effectively applied to reduce medical billing costs, especially at the stages of electronic submission and scrubbing. However, excess focus on reducing the costs of individual process components, while ignoring total billing quality, exposes the medical practice to a significant financial downside. Quantification of billing quality, and its inclusion into the price-performance equation of billing service, yields a more comprehensive financial picture and better decisions about billing service selection and management. Such an approach also results in substantially higher remittance and better regulatory compliance. However, it is only effective subject to billing performance guarantees and transparency.

The traditional sequence of management steps to rationalize medical practice billing and reduce its costs requires the physician to invest in processes, personnel, and technology:

1. Study your denials to eliminate errors by using claims-

scrubbing software.

2. Educate your front-end employees about the billing process, and know how to be a part of it.
3. Investigate tools for electronic submission, and take advantage of technology.
4. Set guidelines for which claims and which dollar amounts merit appeals.
5. Provide patients with clear payment policies up front.

ROI in Claims Processing Technology

For illustration, consider the case of a three-office practice with 17 internists and a panel of 20,000 patients, quite similar to Potomac Physician Associates (Donato, 2003) in Bethesda, MD, which, in 2002, brought their claims submission and practice management services in-house. Assuming that three full-time equivalent persons (FTEs) worked in billing and used Vericle's technology, the costs would be about $120,000 for personnel and $36,000 for technology. For reference, Vericle technology performs comprehensive claim validation, patient demographics and eligibility tests prior to a visit, electronic claim submission, and comprehensive reporting for follow-up, etc. Additionally, by using Vericle technology, 98% of claims are now clean, adding further value for the investment in claims processing technology. In this case, billing costs add up to $156,000 annually (Figure 11).

This is a significant accomplishment in terms of billing processing costs, because without advanced technology, the same practice may need at least seven FTEs, at cost of $280,000.

Accordingly, the arrangement prior to installing the Vericle technology cost at least $292,000 (assuming one-third of the cost for an alternative, albeit inferior, billing package). Thus, an investment of $36,000 in superior technology saved at least $136,000, which is obviously an impressive ROI.

Figure 11. ROI in Billing Technology

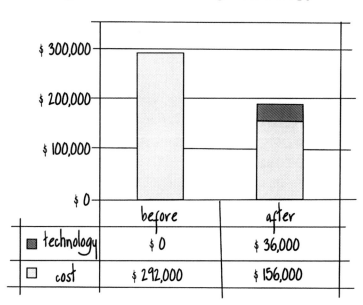

Investing in superior technology reduces claims processing costs.

However, this approach does not account for the entire spectrum of costs associated with an in-house billing approach. It ignores the total revenue aspect of the billing function, which is its ultimate purpose.

Estimated Losses Due to Poor Billing Quality

To receive a more comprehensive perspective, let's compute the total losses generated by uncollected payments. We'll proceed by establishing a convenient baseline and figuring out a way to approximate the losses.

In our experience, the likelihood of payment shrinks dramatically with time. With a few exceptions, the unpaid claims for more than four months are eventually forfeited—hence the importance of A/R beyond 120 days. Therefore, to compute the total losses, we must start with computing the total revenue and then use the days in accounts receivable as a proxy for the underpayment.

For the case study in hand, we estimate the total practice revenue by assuming average physician revenue of $300,000, which, for 17 physicians, adds up to a total of $5,100,000. Next, since the stated percentage of clean claims for electronic submission is about average (98%), we will also assume an average nationwide A/R beyond 120 days, which currently stands at about 17.7% (Lowes, 2004). This number indicates that the amount of losses on the billings of $5,100,000 approaches $902,700. Even if 40% of that A/R were eventually collected, we would still face a revenue loss of $541,620 (Figure 12).

Figure 12. In-house Billing Cost Distribution

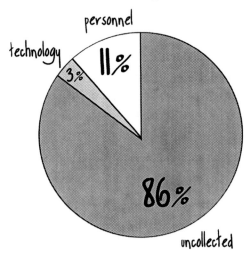

Improving collections quality yields significant benefits over any potential cost savings.

Therefore, while the practice saved $136,000 on personnel, it still lost an estimated $541,620 on billing quality, despite the newly installed technology.

The lesson of this illustration is that the costs of the billing function may be grossly underestimated because of the following common pitfalls:

- **Pitfall #1** – Focus on the costs of individual components of the billing function instead of computing the bottom-line cost to the practice.
- **Pitfall #2** – Underestimate the costs of these components (for personnel costs, these can be benefits, sickness, management, replacement, education, and vacations).
- **Pitfall #3** – Focus on the numbers or quality of claims instead of dollars billed and paid.

An alternative approach, oriented to the bottom line, guarantees improved revenue before spending a dime:

1. Measure your current percentage of A/R beyond 120 days, and assume (for the sake of conservative management) that the money is lost.
2. Find a billing service provider with significantly higher performance levels than your own solution.
3. Base your management decisions on total cost/performance metrics.

Price-Performance Computation

A billing service provider with guaranteed performance levels will typically charge a percentage of payments. This approach aligns the interests of the biller and the physician, and it results in dramatically lower A/R beyond 120 days, often as low as 4% or even 2%. In this case, the difference in remittance between the two approaches amounts to $463,020, or 9.08%, more to the bottom line (Figure 13).

Note that billing quality is a key component of the billing cost computation, and the decision to outsource the billing service is based on a multifold improvement in billing quality. Such an improvement must be so great that only a billing provider specialist can create and maintain the required volumes and economies of scale. Therefore, one should consider outsourcing only after due diligence establishes that the billing provider delivers superior performance, the difference in performance is quantifiable and significant enough for bottom-line growth, and such performance can be verified independently and continuously. A rule of thumb is that the new combined percentage of fees and uncollected revenue must stay below in-house A/R (billing quality measured in terms of the percentage of the billed amount in A/R beyond 120 days).

Additional Benefits of Outsourced Billing

Note also that by outsourcing to the right billing service provider, the practice liberates itself from multiple additional issues associated with the process, personnel, and technology aspects of billing. Specifically, the only remaining billing function for the practice owners is the periodic review of cash flow and accounts receivable—in other words, an entirely bottom-line-driven supervision. There's no need to micromanage the submission process, reconcile rejections, appeal to the payers, etc. Similarly, there's no more need to manage the billing employee team—their vacations, sick days, benefits, teamwork, and turnover. Finally,

Figure 13. Comprehensive Comparison of In-house and Outsourced Billing

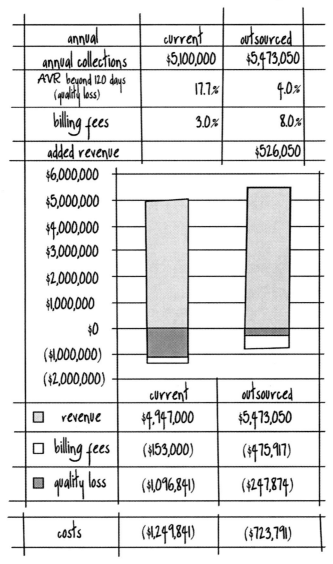

annual	current	outsourced
annual collections	$5,100,000	$5,473,050
AVR beyond 120 days (quality loss)	17.1%	4.0%
billing fees	3.0%	8.0%
added revenue		$526,050

	current	outsourced
▢ revenue	$4,947,000	$5,473,050
▢ billing fees	($153,000)	($475,917)
▣ quality loss	($1,096,841)	($247,874)
costs	($1,249,841)	($723,791)

Improved billing quality yields added revenue
despite higher billing fees.

there's no more need to deal with any technology issues—such as installation, maintenance, backups, disaster recovery, HIPAA compliance, and upgrades.

Sensitivity Analysis

Previous analysis shows that total cost of billing depends on uncollected revenue. Therefore, billing method and vendor selection decision (in-house vs. outsourced) depend on the difference in remittance quality. A basic decision rule can be formulated as

If $R_o + RF - R_oF < R_i - C_P - C_T$
Then the practice should consider billing function outsourcing (Table 3)

Table 3. Decision Rule Parameters	
Parameter	**Meaning**
R	Total billed revenue
R_o	Quality of the outsourced vendor, measured in terms of A/R beyond 120 days
R_i	Quality of the in-house function, measured in terms of A/R beyond 120 days
F	Outsourced fee
C_P	Cost of in-house personnel
C_T	Cost of in-house technology

Note that both the billing service providers and the practices can use the above rule to establish the limit values for service rationalization as well as fee negotiation. For instance, if our illustration physician group improves its in-house remittance quality so that its A/R beyond 120 days drops from 17.7% down to below 8.34%, then, subject to remaining constant parameters, the practice will do better by keeping the billing function in-house. On the other hand, if the group quality is at 17.7% or higher, then any fee below 17.7% is worth paying as long as the provider guarantees the A/R beyond 120 days below 4%. Finally, if the practice prefers establishing a fee limit, then it may be used to determine the required quality guarantee. For instance, if the provider agrees to pay a fee at 12%, then any A/R below 10% benefits the provider.

Pricing of Outsourced Billing Service

Given practice revenue, internal costs, and quality rates for in-house billing, we can now plot the values for optimal billing rate as a percentage of total revenues and a function of outsourced service quality. Assuming outsourced quality ranges between 2% and 18% and a constant in-house quality rate of 17%, 12%, and 8%, the optimal billing graph takes the form depicted in Figure 14.

Figure 14. Billing Quality and Service Pricing

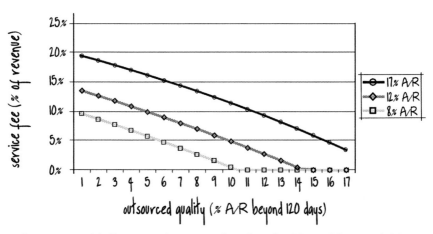

Outsourced billing quality rate family of 17%, 12%, and 8%.

Summary

We draw three lessons about how to compute the cost of billing and select a better billing service provider:

1. **Costs** – Billing costs may be grossly underestimated because of neglect of uncollected revenue for
   a. in-house billing
   b. outsourced billing

2. **Decision making**
   a. The financial difference between in-sourcing and outsourcing may be huge, depending on the difference in respective performance.
   b. The billing service provider selection must be based, first of all, on billing quality.

3. **Selection** – Prior to hiring an outsourced service provider, make sure that the provider
   a. guarantees billing quality
   b. provides tools for continuous quality verification (transparency)

Chapter 29

Dilemma of Outsourced Billing Service

Statistics show that both in-house and outsourced billing services may deliver superior or inadequate billing performance.
On one hand, only 5.66% of "better-performing practices" outsource their billing. In other words, the vast majority of "better-
performing practices" achieve adequate billing performance in-
house. On the other hand, less than 83% of payments are paid to
an average practice within the first four months of the date of
service. Worse, 59% of in-house billers do not review the explanations of benefits, and 55% of billers have never appealed a denied claim. In other words, the average medical practice delivers
almost one-fifth of its services for free because in-house billing
fails to provide adequate payment performance (Annual Medical
Billing Salary and Statistics Survey, 2004; Maguire, 2000).

Can an outsourced electronic medical billing software and
service improve or expedite payments and reduce costs? This
chapter revisits key arguments for and against outsourced billing
in light of the increasing complexity and regulatory scrutiny of
billing processes.

Arguments FOR Outsourcing

1. Improved billing performance in spite of continuously reduced fee schedules, growing billing complexity, frequent audits, and payer consolidation into larger networks
2. Extra time to focus on patient care and/or practice development
3. Reduced operating costs

Billing performance improvement is typically measured in reduced accounts receivable, faster median payment, and reduced underpayment and denial ratios. The practice owner uses the extra time for family, patient care, or practice development. The cost gains are typically measured in the saved salaries and benefits of billing personnel who are no longer needed. It's important to keep in mind that a 10% improvement in overall billing quality means 10 times more to the practice's bottom line than a 1% reduction in billing fees. Therefore, if an outsourced billing service provider is able to significantly improve billing performance, the cost reduction may be marginal in comparison to a total contribution to the practice's bottom line.

Arguments AGAINST Outsourcing

1. Upcoding risk
2. Deficient follow-up

If the billing service charges a percentage of total collections, then, according to the upcoding argument, the service has an incentive to use a CPT code with a higher return, which often contradicts medical notes on hand. As the practice owner is ultimately responsible for the medical claims, such a billing service exposes the owner to upcoding felony charges. On the other hand, the practice owner with an in-house billing operation pays flat salaries to the billing personnel, eliminating the incentive for upcoding.

The deficient denial follow-up argument is a variation of a zero-sum argument. It's based on an assumption that a billing service provider's capacity for a follow-up process is limited and that clients must compete for it. A win for one client must necessarily be a loss for another. By driving such follow-up activity down to zero, the billing service provider wins at the expense of every one of its clients. The larger the client base of the billing service, the more it wins, while the payments to each individual client continue to shrink because of the increasingly bad follow-up.

In the extreme case, when the electronic billing software and service provider has no ability to follow up at all (for instance, when the service is offered at excessively low prices, such as 4%), the provider ends up losing twice—first, by paying a fee for the automatically paid claims, and then, by receiving no service on underpayments and leaving a major part of earned compensation to the insurer. On the other hand, the practice with an in-house billing operation has all of its billing capacity focused on follow-up for a single practice, so the in-house billing service will necessarily bring better results than the outsourced service.

Counter-Argument Analysis

- The upcoding argument is irrelevant for doctors who code themselves by using an electronic, or even a paper, superbill. Next, if the biller is expected to code, then the practice owner must ensure that its compliance process protects both the practice and the billing service. The penalties for noncompliance have been steadily escalating in the last decade; today, those penalties include financial, licensure, and imprisonment aspects. A practice without a compliance process faces a higher risk of failing a random post-payment audit and paying higher penalties than a practice with a formal compliance process in place. Once a comprehensive process is implemented fully and reliably, the practice owner eliminates major risk, regardless of having the billing service in-house or outsourced.

- Measuring billing quality exposes the fallacy of the zero-sum argument. If a medical practice that performs in-house billing demonstrates a lower percentage of accounts receivable beyond 120 days than the national average, 17.7% (Moore, 2003), then its billers do have better follow-up performance, and the comparative analysis reduces to comparing total in-house costs to total billing office fees. Again, since a 10% improvement in overall billing quality means 10 times more to the practice's bottom line than a 1% reduction in billing fees, an outsourced billing service provider that charges a percentage of total collections has a larger incentive to improve overall payment performance than to sell the service to another medical practice.

- Recent progress made by industry leaders, in terms of overall billing quality and included services, confirms this analysis. Aggressive up-front claim scrubbing, real-time compliance analysis, and automated denial follow-up are just a few activities provided by modern

Vericle-type billing software to enable continuous improvement of billing performance in step with the growing scale and number of clients. Other important developments are billing workflow integration with practice management tools—including patient scheduling, electronic medical records (EMR) or SOAP notes—and real-time reporting and alert generation.

Summary

In conclusion, abstract arguments for and against outsourced electronic medical billing are pointless, because both sides can be shown right or wrong, depending on specific and quantitative performance measures. Practice owners must establish objective performance and compliance criteria, and they must use them systematically and within the individual practice's context when addressing the question of outsourced medical billing.

Chapter 30

Nine Criteria for Best SaaS

Software as a Service (SaaS) pushes the limits of outsourcing and reduces the exorbitant costs of specialized practice management software. An SaaS model is available for all aspects of chiropractic clinic management—including scheduling, billing, and SOAP note documentation, which are mission-critical for high-quality healthcare, practice building, and regulatory compliance.

What is Software as a Service?

Software as a Service (SaaS) is a logical step in the progression from build to buy to subscribe, and it's a manifestation of a major software trend toward service-oriented architecture (SOA). SaaS is the software industry term for delivery of software products and services over a network (typically the Internet) under a subscription business model.

The increasing reliability of the Internet, coupled with the availability of completely integrated practice management and billing software, creates supportive conditions for the "pay as you go" business model. SaaS liberates the users in two significant ways:

1. SaaS requires no large up-front investment in hardware and software licenses on the part of the user.

2. SaaS shifts the onus of systems management from the user to the SaaS vendor, including the following:
   a. Internet connectivity, bandwidth, and routers
   b. Servers for web server software, email, and firewalls
   c. Capacity management
   d. Redundancy management
   e. Application upgrade management

In financial management terms, the SaaS proposition is equivalent to turning capital expense into operating expense, which translates into the following:

1. Better balance sheets
2. Lower risk, especially during the period of rapid technology innovation on one hand and practice-building stages on the other hand

SaaS differs from application service providers (ASPs) in two ways: domain expertise and software development skills. While ASP vendors have developed primarily hardware and systems expertise and offered foreign business applications, SaaS vendors are experts in the specific application domain.

SaaS Vendor Selection

For the manager of a chiropractic clinic, the main challenge could be the integration of newer applications with the subscribed SaaS application. SaaS integration platforms (SIPs) are a popular way to handle the integration challenge. An SIP, such as Vericle, offers a suite of integrated applications such as patient relationship management, patient scheduling, SOAP notes, and billing.

A chiropractic clinic in search of an SaaS vendor must focus on the following factors:

1. **Functionality** – Does the application deliver the required functionality?
2. **Training** – Will the vendor provide sufficient application training?
3. **Third-party application interface** – Does the application work with applications already deployed in the office? What requirements must be satisfied if you decide to purchase another application later?
4. **Performance** – How do you measure application performance? Are formal performance metrics available continuously?
5. **HIPAA compliance** – What controls are in place to enable access on a "need to see" basis only? Is every access instance logged using a secure mechanism?
6. **Service level agreement (SLA)** – What minimum service levels does the vendor guarantee to the client? What are the penalties for violating the SLA?
7. **Data ownership** – Who owns the data?
8. **Disaster recovery** – How long would it take to recover from a disaster? Is a secondary data center

available 24/7?

9. **Disengagement procedures** – How long is data available upon severing the relationship? Who is responsible for data transfer to the new vendor?

Chapter 31

Lockbox Selection Process

A lockbox helps a medical practice streamline HIPAA-compliant mail processing and same-day check deposits. Electronic access to scanned documents, including EOBs, simplifies key office and billing processes and achieves multiple benefits:

- **Reliability** – Better revenue-cycle reliability via elimination of dependency on staff or on the billing service to handle checks.
- **Transparency** – Allows bi-directional verification of check deposits between the bank and the billing service. The doctor can personally verify deposits 24/7 via a secure Internet connection. There are no lost checks.
- **Billing efficiency** – Faster and better-controlled submission of secondary claims.
- **Patient service efficiency** – Simpler and faster resolution of patient account inquiries and disputes.
- **Added interest revenue** – Automated or semi-

automated posting of insurance and patient payments. Checks are deposited upon arrival. Deposits are automatically invested (via automatic sweep) in a money market account that earns interest. The doctor's money is never idle.

Lockbox Operation

1. Practice mail arrives directly to the lockbox service.
2. Lockbox service
   a. All mail is opened and archived in a document management system, including scanning and indexing for future retrieval.
   b. Images are available to the practice or billing service via a secure, encrypted website.
   c. All checks received that day are deposited.
   d. Practice administrative staff has direct access to web-driven interfaces for mail, check queries, and reports.

Lockbox Implementation

A lockbox service is typically offered by two kinds of providers:

1. Large-scale, Vericle-like billing service vendor as part of service
2. Specialized financial institution (e.g., bank)

Lockbox Selection

1. **HIPAA compliance** – Can the service guarantee ac-

cess only on a "need to know" basis and only to qualified staff? Are all required privacy and security measures in place? Is there a solid disaster recovery capability and process?

2. **Quality assurance process** – What measures are taken to ensure timely error identification, correction, and tracking? Is there sufficient QA (quality assurance) process transparency to allow the practice owner complete control of mail and checks?

3. **Intuitive user interface** – How many steps are required to find a letter, EOB, or check? What are mail and check indexing parameters?

4. **Batch interfaces** – Is there a convenient way to download all or partial content of the document management system for upload to other systems (such as a billing system) or to an alternative lockbox provider facility?

5. **Time frames** – How long does it take to open mail, scan it into a document management system, and deposit a check? What is the time horizon for archived image storage? What is the time period for storage of original paper before shredding?

Lockbox Complexities

1. The lockbox must be fully implemented. A partial implementation only increases management complexity.
2. The lockbox adds a headache for payers. All payers

need to change your mailing address, adding the like-lihood of errors during the transition period.

Summary

In summary, lockbox services lower administrative costs, increase staff productivity, and close collection cycles faster. A more efficiently run practice and happier staff mean more satisfied patients.

Chapter 32

Problem Tracking

Processes involving large volumes of complex billing transactions require effective mechanisms for problem assignment and tracking. Without such mechanisms, billing personnel cannot be held accountable for problem resolution, resulting in a loss of revenue and increased compliance risk. While the medical billing industry has developed specialized systems and processes for the resolution of content problems, little attention has been paid to the methodology for billing process problem resolution. This chapter outlines a process and a technology for integrated billing process problem resolution.

Tracking Methodologies

Medical billing exceptions can be categorized into content and process problems. Content problems have to do with claim content and patterns of processed claims, such as terminology, medical necessity, patient eligibility, denial follow-up, and regulatory billing compliance. Process problems have to do with claim formatting, system interfaces, entry of patient demographics, posting of charges and payments, printing and mailing/faxing of required information, provider interaction procedures, systems access, and HIPAA compliance.

While streamlining and transparency are important attributes for the resolution of both kinds of problems, the required processes and systems are very different. Content problems tend to be specialized, and they therefore lend themselves to a more structured, almost template-driven solution approach. Process problems, in contrast to content problems, tend to cover a wide variety of knowledge domains, precluding specialization.

The difference in solution methodologies drives the difference in problem tracking. For content problem resolution methodology, the reader is advised to consult the chapters on metrics, Straight-Through Billing, and billing transparency. The remainder of this chapter focuses on process problem tracking.

Billing Process Problem Tracking

A general-purpose tracking system allows for opening a problem ticket, its assignment to specific team member, its reassignment or escalation, its change of status (depending on the problem resolution stage), convenient reporting about sets of tickets in different states or assigned to different team members, and continuous notification of everybody involved about the change of status. Therefore, such a tracking system (e.g., web-based TrackLogix) is constructed around three basic reports, a notification mechanism, and a concept of ticket.

Problem Tracking Reports

These reports show the following:

1. Tickets you owe to others
2. Tickets owed to you
3. Status – a summary table of the team participants with statistics of tickets in different states

Other reports may show and compare individual productivity and responsiveness.

Problem Notification

For transparency, the team members must be continuously aware of every problem resolution status. The simplest way to maintain such awareness is to send an email to every team member about every status change event of a problem ticket. Other popular notification media include paging and short message service (SMS) calls. More sophisticated methods involve selective notification based on the nature of the event or the person assigned to problem resolution.

Problem Ticket

The problem ticket has the following data elements:

1. **Subject** – Short description of the problem

2. **Owner** – Name of the employee responsible for issue resolution

3. **Requestor** – Name of the manager who assigned the issue to the employee

4. **Date** – Date the issue was identified and documented

5. **Scheduled** – Date (time) by which this issue must be resolved

6. **Body** – Detailed issue description

7. **Log** – Time-stamped and owner-stamped history of all documentation, including
   a. Escalation – Issues may be escalated to upper management via TrackLogix by simply changing the owner
   b. Priority change
   c. Status change
   d. Date change
   e. Owner change
   f. Specific action taken to resolve the issue

8. **Priority** – Ranking of relative issue importance among other issues on the same workbench

9. **Status**
   a. Open for new issue
   b. Pending resolution and waiting for approval
   c. Closed (resolved) and approved

Summary

Vericle-like Straight-Through Billing (STB) systems automate the majority of billing transactions and focus manual follow-up on exceptions. A formal web-based process and problem-tracking system, such as TrackLogix, provides accountability, which is based on a precise account of all process problems and their resolution status. With such a tracking system, all problems are visible to every process participant. An increased level of personal accountability promotes teamwork, increases client satisfaction, and assists in streamlining the process.

For more information about problem resolution transparency and its four attributes—including universality, continuity, ubiquity, and scalability—read Chapter 23 about medical billing transparency.

Glossary of Billing Terms

Account Number: A unique number that's assigned to patients each time they visit the hospital. A new number is issued for each visit.

Adjustment: A portion of the patient's hospital bill that's adjusted due to a contract between the provider and the individual insurance companies.

Amount Not Covered: A portion of the patient's hospital bill that the insurance company will not pay. It may include deductibles, coinsurances, and charges for noncovered services.

Amount Payable by Plan: The amount the insurance plan pays or covers for the patient's treatment, less any deductibles, coinsurance, or charges for noncovered services.

Benefit: The services that are covered under the insurance plan.

COBRA Insurance: Health insurance coverage that patients can purchase when they're no longer employed, or when they're awaiting coverage from a new insurance plan to begin. Coverage may be purchased for up to 18 months from the termination of employment. It's generally more expensive than insurance provided through the employer, but less expensive than insurance purchased as an individual policy.

Coinsurance: The percentage of coverage not covered under insurance benefits. For example, the policy may cover 80% of charges. The coinsurance/patient portion would be the remaining 20%.

Co-payment/Co-pay: A set fee established by the insurance company for a specific type of visit. This amount is due from the guarantor. This information is routinely located on the insurance card and is different according to the type of visit. For example, emergency room visit: $50; inpatient stay: $100; physician office visit: $20.

Date of Service (DOS): The date(s) when the patient was provided healthcare services. For an inpatient stay, the dates of service are the date of admission through the discharge date. For outpatient services, the date of service is the date of the office visit.

Deductible: An amount that must be met on an annual basis that's established by the insurance company and the benefit plan.

Electronic Claims Clearinghouse: An electronic claims clearinghouse accepts insurance claims and submits them to payers. Clearinghouses reduce the complexity of provider-payer connectivity. A clearinghouse is a necessary component of a seamless (built-in) system that allows a practice or billing service to submit all claims electronically and have them validated online and in almost real-time.

A clearinghouse delivers economies of scale in two important ways:

1. Saves the billing service or practice the cost of direct connection to payers
2. Expedites the revenue cycle by testing the validity of submitted claims prior to delivering them to payers

The clearinghouse receives claims, checks them for completeness and accuracy, forwards valid claims to payers, and notifies the submission source about any problems, expediting the correction process and claim resubmission.

Given N providers and M payers, a complete network of all N providers submitting claims to all M payers requires N x M connections. A clearinghouse, connected to all providers and payers, reduces the number of connections down to M + N.

Explanation of Benefits (EOB): This is a notice the patient receives from the insurance company after the claim for healthcare services has been processed. It explains the amounts billed, paid, denied, discounted, and not covered, and the amount owed by the patient. The EOB may also communicate information needed by the insured in order to process the claim.

Guarantor: The person responsible for payment of the bill.

Health Maintenance Organization (HMO): An insurance plan that has contracted with providers to provide healthcare services at a discounted rate. These services will require prior certification, authorization, and/or referrals.

Managed Care: An insurance plan that has a contract with hospitals, physicians, and other healthcare providers.

Medicaid: A state-administered, federal- and state-funded insurance plan for low-income families who have limited or no insurance.

Medicare: A health insurance program for people age 65 and older, some people with disabilities under age 65, and people with end-stage renal disease (ESRD).

Medicare Part A (Hospital Insurance): Healthcare coverage for inpatient stays at participating hospitals.

Medicare Part B (Medical Insurance): Healthcare coverage for doctors' services, outpatient hospital care, and some other medical services that Part A does not cover, such as the services of physical and occupational therapists and some home healthcare.

Medigap: Medicare Supplemental Insurance available by private insurance companies that pay for some services not covered by Medicare A or B, including deductibles and coinsurance amounts.

Noncovered Services: Services not covered under the patient's insurance plan. These charges are the patient's responsibility to pay.

Out-of-Network Provider/Nonparticipating Provider: Provider that's not part of the insurance plan's network of contracted providers. Generally, insurance plans pay less for services at an out-of-network provider, and the guarantor has higher out-of-pocket costs.

Out-of-Pocket Cost: The amount that the patient pays until the benefit coverage reaches 100%.

Payer: Insurance company that pays for benefits.

Point-of-Service Plan: An insurance plan that allows the patient to choose doctors and hospitals without first having to get a referral from the primary care physician.

Pre-Authorization Number: Authorization given by a health plan for a member to obtain services from a healthcare provider. This is commonly required for hospital services.

Pre-Certification Number: A number obtained from the insurance company by doctors and hospitals. This number will represent the agreement by the insurance plan that the service has been approved. This is not a guarantee of payment.

Preferred Provider Organization (PPO): An insurance plan that has a contract with providers to provide healthcare services at a discounted rate. These services may require prior certification, authorization, and/or referrals.

Provider: Healthcare service provider.

Referral: Approval or consent by a primary care doctor for a patient to see a certain specialist or receive certain services.

Subscriber: The person responsible for payment of premiums or whose employment is the basis for eligibility for a health plan membership.

References

Aalseth, P. T. (1999). *Codebusters: Quick Guide to Coding and Billing Compliance for Medical Practices*. Gaithersberg, MD: Aspen.

Bruderlin, F. (2003). TriCity Medical Center Gives Its Cash Flow Problem a Shot in the Arm. *Healthcare Biller: The Communication Network for America's Health Care Billers, 12*(1).

Buppert, C. (2005). *The Primary Care Provider's Guide to Compensation and Quality: How to Get Paid and Not Get Sued*. Sudbury, MA: Jones and Bartlett.

Burgos, M., Johnson, D., & Keogh, J. (2006). *Medical Billing & Coding Demystifi*ed. New York: McGraw-Hill.

Capra, B., Lirov, Y., & Randolph, J. (2006, December). The "Business" of Healthcare Provider Audits – How Payers Are Getting Away with Practice Murder. *Today's Chiropractic*, 60–62.

Delman, I. (2002). *The Business of Chiropractic: How to Prosper After Startup* (2nd edition). Dandridge, TN: Business of Chiropractic Publications.

Donato, S. (2003, April). Three Steps to Fewer Denials. Getting Claims Management Under Control. *Physicians Practice*. Retrieved August 7, 2007, from http://www.physicianspractice .com/index.cfm?fuseaction=articles.details&articleID=397

Fuhrmans, V. (2007, February 14). Billing Battle: Fights Over Health Claims Spawn a New Arms Race; Insurers and Doctors Are Spending Billions; Firms Help Both Sides. *Wall Street Journal* (Eastern edition), p. A1.

Hashim, M., Franks, P., & Fiscella, K. (2001). Effectiveness of Telephone Reminders in Improving Rate of Appointments Kept at an Outpatient Clinic: A Randomized Controlled Trial. *Journal of the American Board of Family Practice, 14*(3), 193–196.

Healthcare Financial Management Association. (2003). *Tip Sheet: Medical Claims Denial Management*. Westchester, IL: Author.

Laub, G., & Lirov, Y. (2006). The Game of Medical Billing in Today's Cardiology Practice, *EP Lab Digest, 6*(4), 8–9.

Lirov, Y. (1997). *Mission-Critical Systems Management*. Upper Saddle River, NJ: Prentice Hall.

Lirov, Y. (2006). 4 Step Denial Management To Improve Performance Of Electronic Medical Billing Software And Service. Retrieved August 2, 2007, from http://ezinearticles.com/?4 -Step-Denial-Management-To-Improve-Performance-Of- Electronic-Medical-Billing-Software-And-Service&id=310321

Lirov, Y. (2006). 5-Step Lockbox Selection for Outsourced Electronic Medical Billing Software and Service. Retrieved August 2, 2007, from http://ezinearticles.com/?5-Step-Lockbox-Selection -for-Outsourced-Electronic-Medical-Billing-Software-and -Service&id=292801

Lirov, Y. (2006). 7-Step Chiropractic Office Billing Precision Software For Result-Driven Patient Care Plan. Retrieved August 2, 2007, from http://ezinearticles.com/?7-Step-Chiropractic -Office-Billing-Precision-Software-For-Result-Driven-Patient -Care-Plan&id=283199

Lirov, Y. (2006). 8-Step Plan for Software and Practice Integration of Electronic Medical Billing Service + SaaS EMR . Retrieved August 2, 2007, from http://ezinearticles.com/?8-Step-Plan-for -Software-and-Practice-Integration-of--Electronic-Medical -Billing-Service-+-SaaS-EMR-&id=319226

Lirov, Y. (2006). Best-Of-Breed Medical Billing Service + SaaS EMR − 8 Software and Practice Transition Challenges. Retrieved August 2, 2007, from http://ezinearticles.com/?Best-Of-Breed -Medical-Billing-Service-+-SaaS-EMR---8-Software-and -Practice-Transition-Challenges&id=317981

Lirov, Y. (2006). Centralized Workflow Management for Outsourced Electronic Medical Billing Service and Software. Retrieved August 2, 2007, from http://ezinearticles.com/ ?Centralized-Workflow-Management-for-Outsourced-Electronic -Medical-Billing-Service-and-Software&id=214866

Lirov, Y. (2006). Chiropractic Office Billing Software And Patient Relationship Management − 9 Criteria For Best SaaS. Retrieved August 2, 2007, from http://ezinearticles.com/?Chiropractic

-Office-Billing-Software-And-Patient-Relationship-Management
---9-Criteria-For-Best-SaaS&id=309747

Lirov, Y. (2006). Computer Aided Patient Scheduling for Improved Medical Billing Service Performance. Retrieved August 2, 2007, from http://ezinearticles.com/?Computer-Aided-Patient-Scheduling-for-Improved-Medical-Billing-Service-Performance&id=236317

Lirov, Y. (2006). Electronic Medical Billing Control with Computer Aided Coding Software. Retrieved August 2, 2007, from http://ezinearticles.com/?Electronic-Medical-Billing-Control-with-Computer-Aided-Coding-Software&id=240570

Lirov, Y. (2006). Electronic Medical Billing Dashboard Software – 9 Performance Indicators For Service Outsourcing. Retrieved August 2, 2007, from http://ezinearticles.com/?Electronic-Medical-Billing-Dashboard-Software---9-Performance-Indicators-For-Service-Outsourcing&id=301114

Lirov, Y. (2006). Electronic Medical Billing OLAP Software for Lost Revenue Discovery. Retrieved August 2, 2007, from http://ezinearticles.com/?Electronic-Medical-Billing-OLAP-Software-for-Lost-Revenue-Discovery&id=248675

Lirov, Y. (2006). Electronic Medical Billing Software and Service Compliance With Pre-Payment And Post-Payment Audits. Retrieved August 2, 2007, from http://ezinearticles.com/?Electronic-Medical-Billing-Software-and-Service-Compliance-With-Pre-Payment-And-Post-Payment-Audits&id=227773

Lirov, Y. (2006). Electronic Medical Billing Software and Service

Performance Metrics. Retrieved August 2, 2007, from http://ezinearticles.com/?Electronic-Medical-Billing-Software-and-Service-Performance-Metrics&id=215620

Lirov, Y. (2006). Electronic Medical Billing Software, HIPAA Compliance, and Role Based Access Control. Retrieved August 2, 2007, from http://ezinearticles.com/?Electronic-Medical-Billing-Software,-HIPAA-Compliance,-and-Role-Based-Access-Control&id=250740

Lirov, Y. (2006). Electronic Straight Through Billing Service and Software Methodology for Medical Practice. Retrieved August 2, 2007, from http://ezinearticles.com/?Electronic-Straight-Through-Billing-Service-and-Software-Methodology-for-Medical-Practice&id=246227

Lirov, Y. (2006). Practice Perfect – 10 Criteria For Best Chiropractic Billing Software And Office Management Solution. Retrieved August 2, 2007, from http://ezinearticles.com/?Practice-Perfect---10-Criteria-For-Best-Chiropractic-Billing-Software-And-Office-Management-Solution&id=306832

Lirov, Y. (2006). Problem Tracking For Outsourced Electronic Medical Billing Software And Service. Retrieved August 2, 2007, from http://ezinearticles.com/?Problem-Tracking-For-Outsourced-Electronic-Medical-Billing-Software-And-Service&id=247225

Lirov, Y. (2006). Relative Value Price-Performance Calculation for Outsourced Electronic Medical Billing Service. Retrieved August 2, 2007, from http://ezinearticles.com/?Relative-Value-Price-Performance-Calculation-for-Outsourced-Electronic

-Medical-Billing-Service&id=206604

Lirov, Y. (2006). Top 3 Electronic Medical Billing Software Methods For No-Show And Missed Appointment Risk Reduction. Retrieved August 2, 2007, from http://ezinearticles.com/?Top-3-Electronic-Medical-Billing-Software-Methods-For-No-Show-And-Missed-Appointment-Risk-Reduction-&id=328056

Lirov, Y. (2006). Top 4 Reports For Patient Relationship Management And Outsourced Chiropractic Office Billing Service. Retrieved August 2, 2007, from http://ezinearticles.com/?Top-4-Reports-For-Patient-Relationship-Management-And-Outsourced-Chiropractic-Office-Billing-Service&id=324869

Lirov, Y. (2006). Top 5 Keys To Physician Interface Dilemma In Electronic Medical Billing And EMR Software Systems. Retrieved August 2, 2007, from http://ezinearticles.com/?Top-5-Keys-To-Physician-Interface-Dilemma-In-Electronic-Medical-Billing-And-EMR-Software-Systems&id=288275

Lirov, Y. (2007). Appointment Reminders for Medical Billing Revenue Protection and Patient Relationship Management. Retrieved August 2, 2007, from http://ezinearticles.com/?Appointment-Reminders-for-Medical-Billing-Revenue-Protection-and-Patient-Relationship-Management&id=459864

Lirov, Y. (2007). Chiropractic Office Workflow In 2025 – Scheduling, Clinical Service, Notes, And Billing Software. Retrieved August 2, 2007, from http://ezinearticles.com/?Chiropractic-Office-Workflow-In-2025---Scheduling,-Clinical-Service,-Notes,-And-Billing-Software&id=425699

Lirov, Y. (2007). Improve Patient Loyalty with Integrated Electronic Medical Billing, Notes, And Scheduling Software. Retrieved August 2, 2007, from http://ezinearticles.com/?Improve-Patient-Loyalty-with-Integrated-Electronic-Medical-Billing,-Notes,-And-Scheduling-Software&id=427289

Lirov, Y. (2007). Intelligent Electronic Medical Billing and SOAP Notes Software Requirements. Retrieved August 2, 2007, from http://ezinearticles.com/?Improve-Patient-Loyalty-with-Integrated-Electronic-Medical-Billing,-Notes,-And-Scheduling-Software&id=427289

Lirov, Y. (2007). Outsourcing Dilemma Of Electronic Medical Billing Software And Service. Retrieved August 2, 2007, from http://ezinearticles.com/?Outsourcing-Dilemma-Of-Electronic-Medical-Billing-Software-And-Service-&id=490193

Lirov, Y. (2007). Top 5 Strategies to Improve OTC Payment Performance With Electronic Medical Billing Software. Retrieved August 2, 2007, from http://ezinearticles.com/?Top-5-Strategies-to-Improve-OTC-Payment-Performance-With-Electronic-Medical-Billing-Software&id=539366

Lowes, R. (2004). Practice Pointers: How to Cut A/R. *Medical Economics, 81*(17), 22. Retrieved August 7, 2007, from http://www.memag.com/memag/article/articleDetail.jsp?id=120970

Maguire, P. (2000, December). Your practice claims denied? Take steps to get what you're owed. *American College of Physicians-American Society of Internal Medicine Observer.* Retrieved August 7, 2007, from http://www.acponline.org/journals/news/dec00/claimsdenied.htm

Marcinko, D. E. (2004). *The Business of Medical Practice: Advanced Profit Maximization Techniques for Savvy Doctors*. New York: Springer.

Medical Association of Billers. (2004). *2004 Annual Medical Billing Salary and Statistics Survey*. Retrieved June 7, 2007, from http://www.e-medbill.com/biller_survey_results.htm

Metcalfe, R. M. (2007, May 7). It's All In Your Head. *Forbes, 179*(10), 52–56. Retrieved August 7, 2007, from http://www.forbes.com/free_forbes/2007/0507/052.html

Moore, C., Wilson-Witherspoon, P., & Probst, J. (2001). Time and Money: Effects of No-Shows at a Family Practice Residency Clinic. *Family Medicine, 33*(7), 522–527.

Moore, P. L. (2007, January). Power to the Payers – Consolidation Puts Insurers in Charge. *Physicians Practice*, 23–30. Retrieved August 7, 2007, from http://www.physicianspractice.com/index/fuseaction/articles.details/articleID/933.htm

Office of Inspector General (OIG). (2006). *Health Care Fraud and Abuse Control Annual Report: Fiscal 2005*. Washington, DC: Author.

Reizer, J. L., & Reizer, S. (2002). *Up and Running – Opening a Chiropractic Office*. Otsego, MI: PageFree.

Rowell, J. C., & Green, M. A. (2005). *Understanding Health Insurance: A Guide to Billing and Reimbursement* (8th edition). Florence, KY: Thomson Delmar Learning.

Saner, R. J., Spindel, M., & Nordeng, A. (2000). *Understanding Compliance: A Program Guide Based on the OIG 2000 Guidance*. Englewood, CO: Medical Group Management Association.

Stechschulte, P. (2003). A Glance into the Future. *Today's Chiropractic, 32*(3), 38–45. Retrieved August 7, 2007, from http://www.todayschiropractic.com/issues/archives/may_jun_03/mj2003_feature_office.html

U. S. Department of Justice, Civil Division. (2005). *Fraud Statistics – October 1, 1986–September 30, 2004*. Washington, DC: Author.

U. S. Government Accountability Office (GAO). *Medicare Spending, Testimony Before the Subcommittee on Health, Committee on Energy and Commerce, House of Representatives*, 110th Cong. (March 6, 2007).

Weinberg, N. (2005, March 14). Envy Engines. *Forbes, 176(5)*. Retrieved August 7, 2007, from http://members.forbes.com/forbes/2005/0314/090sidebar2.html

Index

ROI. *See* return on investment
role-based access control
(RBAC), 97, 101, 102
SaaS. *See* Software as a Service
SaaS integration platform (SIP),
158
schedule. *See* scheduler
scheduler, xvi, xxv, 16, 17, 27, 34,
35, 37, 39, 41, 47, 48, 49, 50,
51, 52, 53, 54, 56, 63, 65, 70,
81, 82, 83, 84, 97, 100, 102,
125, 128, 132, 152, 155, 156,
158, 167
scheduling. *See* scheduler
security, xxiii, 45, 95, 97, 98,
100, 101, 162
service level agreement (SLA),
158
service-oriented architecture
(SOA), 156
short message service (SMS), 166
SIP. *See* SaaS integration
platform
SLA. *See* service level agreement
SMS. *See* short message service
SOA. *See* service-oriented
architecture
SOAAP, 42, 43
SOAP, xvi, xxv, 27, 35, 36, 41, 42,
47, 73, 74, 75, 76, 77, 83, 84,
122, 123, 155, 156, 158
Software as a Service (SaaS), 5,
45, 57, 79, 80, 102, 109, 139,
156, 157, 158
SQL, 110, 134, 135, 136

STB. *See* Straight-Through
Billing
STP. *See* Straight-Through
Processing
Straight-Through Billing (STB),
34, 37, 38, 39, 40, 165, 167
Straight-Through Processing
(STP), xxiv, 5, 39, 109
Structured Query Language. *See*
SQL
subjective, 42, 76, 112
Subjective, Objective,
Assessment, and Plan. *See*
SOAP
superbill, xxii, 45, 66, 68, 69, 70,
84, 153
touch screen, 35, 36
TrackLogix, 83, 131, 165, 167
transparency, 26, 34, 37, 38, 44,
56, 58, 100, 109, 117, 118, 119,
120, 141, 150, 160, 162, 165,
166, 168
treatment plan, 43, 76
underpayment, xv, xvi, xxi, xxiii,
3, 8, 12, 13, 14, 16, 17, 23, 28,
37, 38, 65, 117, 131, 132, 134,
135, 136, 137, 144, 152, 153
validation, 38, 39, 63, 77, 130,
142, 170
voice recognition, 87
workbench, 34, 63, 84, 167
workflow, xvi, xvii, 26, 27, 33, 34,
35, 37, 38, 39, 40, 41, 61, 62,
63, 64, 81, 82, 88, 89, 121, 155
zero-sum argument, 153, 154

About the Author

Yuval Lirov, PhD, is the author of *Mission-Critical Systems Management* (Prentice Hall, 1997), inventor of patents in artificial intelligence and computer security, and CEO of Vericle.net Distributed Practice Management and Billing Technologies. Prior to co-founding Vericle, Lirov managed technology at Lehman Brothers, Salomon Smith Barney, and Bell Laboratories. The hallmark of his career has been the introduction of economies of scale and improved service productivity. As a Lehman Brothers senior vice president in charge of technology infrastructure firmwide, he developed Straight-Through Processing systems for the Lehman index production. Lirov earned his doctorate in systems science and mathematics under the guidance of Professor E. Y. Rodin at Washington University in St. Louis.

Printed in the United States
114484LV00004B/196-198/A